GW00360534

THE WI B
MEAT
COOKERY
Over 100 recipes tried and tested
by the Women's Institute

ANGELA MOTTRAM

EBURY
PRESS

ACKNOWLEDGEMENTS

Illustrated by James Farrant
Edited by Suzanne Luchford
Designed by Julia Golding
Cover photography by James Jackson

Published by Ebury Press
Division of The National Magazine Company Limited
Colquhoun House
27–37 Broadwick Street
London W1V 1FR

ISBN 0 85223 573 9

First published 1986

© Copyright 1986 by WI Books Ltd

All rights reserved. No part of this publication may be
reproduced, stored in a retrieval system, or transmitted in
any form or by any means, electronic, mechanical,
photocopying, recording or otherwise without prior
permission of the copyright owner.

Filmset by
D. P. Media Ltd, Hitchin, Hertfordshire

Reproduced, printed and bound in Great Britain by
Hazell, Watson & Viney Ltd,
Member of the BPCC Group, Aylesbury, Bucks

CONTENTS

INTRODUCTION

For centuries meat has been the centre of culinary art in many different cultures, and is closely linked with many customs and traditions. 'Roast beef of old England' is famed abroad, and research shows that over 90 per cent of the population still feel that a 'proper meal' should contain meat, and for a great number that meal will be 'meat and two veg'. In Britain the average family spends 30 per cent of its total food bill on meat. With such a financial investment, it obviously makes sense to use meat to its best advantage. Knowing more about meat and its potential may be of assistance in economising while still providing interesting, nutritionally good meals for the family, or in creating a culinary masterpiece for a special occasion. This book should help to achieve both.

Today there is probably a greater awareness of nutritional values and product quality than ever before. More and more people are concerned with the importance of maintaining a healthy diet and are eager for information and advice. Unfortunately there is a great deal of conflicting material published and the consumer is often very confused about the issues. The recent nutritional guidelines, which have emerged in several reports from various medical and scientific committees, are that, as a nation, we would be much healthier, if we modified our diet. The recommendations are that we should eat less fat overall, and reduce the percentage of saturated fat (from animal sources), using unsaturated fats and oils (vegetable sources) instead; reduce our sugar and salt intake and increase the dietary fibre in our diet. A further recommendation is that we should increase the percentage of vegetable protein we eat; this would automatically increase the fibre intake as the main sources of vegetable protein (nuts, pulse vegetables, beans and wholegrain cereals) are all high in fibre and low in vegetable oil content. How do these recommendations fit in with meat eating?

Meat does not contain sugar or salt, so providing we do not add a great deal during cooking this is not a problem. Salt is not required in cooking, except for flavour (other than in bread making, where it is necessary for a good texture). Increasingly people are finding that they can cut down slowly on the amount of salt in their food, eventually leaving it out altogether. It is amazing what a delicious flavour some foods have when not masked by salt.

The recipes in this book do not require salt, unless stated, although all can be seasoned to taste, which may include salt, pepper or your favourite flavourings. Other flavouring is often required to compensate for the lack of salt; herbs, spices, tomato ketchup and many others can be used for this purpose.

When cutting down on fat, especially animal fat, meat consumption must be considered although it accounts for only a quarter of the saturated fat in our diets. Over the last few years the meat industry has appreciated the consumer's requirement for leaner meat, and the breeding of quickly maturing animals, slaughtering at a younger age, better butchery techniques with presale trimming, have all contributed to much leaner meat being available. It is up to the consumer to look around and choose the meat required. With greater demand the meat industry will continue to respond and produce a product that will sell.

The farmers, producers and butchers are playing their part, but there is plenty the consumer can do. If the meat is not already trimmed, this should be done before cooking. Add little or no fat during cooking; this may mean adapting your usual methods to prevent drying out, but foil or covered containers can help. Prefrying is not necessary before making stews etc, and can be left out, or a minimum of vegetable oil used. The recipes in this book tend to do the latter; readers can opt for leaving that stage out if they wish. Mince and bacon can be cooked in their own fat provided they are heated slowly at the beginning. Leaving out the browning stage may require added flavouring to compensate. Wherever possible, grill rather than fry and drain food well if fried or roasted.

What is meat?

Meat is the flesh or muscle of animals, with its associated fat, and in its wider meaning includes any part of an animal normally consumed. In Britain this usually means the produce from cattle, giving veal and beef, from sheep, giving lamb and mutton, and from pigs, giving pork and bacon, along with offal such as liver, kidney etc from these animals.

Meat is also used to mean the flesh from poultry and game, but that is fully dealt with in *The WI Book of Poultry and Game*. A second book of meat cookery is planned for the future which will cover offal and sausage cookery.

Methods of cooking meat

Meat is cooked to add distinctive flavour, to make it more tender and to make it look more appetising. The choice of cooking method depends largely on the amount of fine gristle contained in the muscles of the cut of meat. In order to get tender meat from muscles with a high proportion of gristle, it is necessary to use long, moist cooking such as stewing, braising or pot roasting. However, cuts with little gristle do not need prolonged, moist cooking and are cooked by the dry methods of roasting, frying and grilling.

Oven roasting. This is in fact baking. The food is cooked in an enclosed space, the oven, and is heated mainly by the convection of hot air. If the joint is very lean, extra fat can be added before roasting, alternatively a roasting bag or foil will prevent drying. An average oven temperature setting is 180°C (350°F) mark 4, which is hot enough to give good browning, but not too much shrinkage. Some people roast at a higher temperature for a shorter time. If potatoes and Yorkshire pudding are to be cooked at the same time, raise the temperature, but cook the meat low in the oven.

Weigh the joint, including stuffing, to calculate the cooking time. The size, shape and percentage of fat all affect cooking time and if using foil or film, will require a little longer.

Beef, rare allow 20 minutes per ½ kg plus 20 minutes over (15 minutes per 1 lb plus 15 minutes over)

Beef, medium allow 25 minutes per ½ kg plus 25 minutes over (20 minutes per 1 lb plus 20 minutes over)

Pork, allow 35 minutes per ½ kg plus 30 minutes over (25 minutes per 1 lb plus 30 minutes over)

Lamb, allow 30 minutes per ½ kg plus 30 minutes over (25 minutes per 1 lb plus 25 minutes over).

The only accurate way to roast meat is to use a meat thermometer, ensuring that the tip is in the centre of the joint and not touching a bone. When the thermometer registers the following temperatures, the meat is cooked.

60°C (140°F) for rare meat
65°C (150°F) for underdone
70°C (160°F) for medium
80°C (180°F) for well done.

Pork should be medium or well done.

Meat, particularly if lean, can be basted during cooking. This is unnecessary with foil or roasting film, which gives a result more like pot-roasting, but is very succulent and juicy.

Spit roasting. In olden times the meat was roasted by being impaled on a rotating spit in front of a glowing fire. This was true roasting, cooking by radiant heat. Nowadays many grills have a rotisserie attachment where the meat is placed on a mechanically operated spit and cooked over or under a direct source of heat. Allow 20 minutes per ½ kg plus 20 minutes over (15 minutes per 1 lb plus 15 minutes over). Pork may require a little longer.

Grilling. This is a quick method of cooking by radiant heat from a preheated gas, electric or charcoal fire or grill. As the heat is fierce, the meat needs to be brushed with oil or butter to prevent drying. Grilling times vary according to the thickness of the meat and the desired degree of cooking. Grilling is only suitable for small tender cuts. As a general guide, for a 2.5 cm (1 in) steak or chop, allow for rare 5 minutes per side, for medium 7 minutes per side and for well done 12 minutes per side.

Frying. As with grilling, frying is only suitable for small tender cuts. Shallow or dry frying, rather than deep-fat frying is used for meat. The fat should be preheated, to avoid greasy results. Turn the meat from time to time and drain well on absorbent paper before serving. Cooking time varies according to the thickness of the meat. Allow 7–10 minutes for 2.5 cm (1 in) steaks, and 4–5 minutes for 1 cm (½ in) steaks.

Stewing. This is the cooking of pieces of meat in liquid, such as water, stock, wine or cider, with added flavourings and/or vegetables, herbs or spices, with or without a thickening agent.

The meat is cooked in 275–575 ml (½–1 pint) of liquid and should only simmer. Stewing can be done in a covered pan, or in a casserole dish in a slow oven, 170°C (325°F) mark 3, when it is usually called casseroling. Joints and large pieces of meat, when covered with liquid and simmered are cooked by boiling. This is in fact stewing.

Stews should be stirred from time to time and not allowed to boil dry. Ensure the lid fits well and top up with stock or water if necessary. Time the cooking from when the stew or cooking liquor comes to the boil, and allow a minimum of 1½ hours. For larger joints, allow 30 minutes per ½ kg (25 minutes per 1 lb) plus an extra 30 minutes. Cuts with a lot of gristle may require longer.

If the meat is covered with water and brought to the boil, it produces a white stew. If the meat and vegetables are fried first, a brown stew is the result.

Braising. After initial browning in hot fat, the meat is

placed on a bed of fried vegetables (called a mirepoix) with just enough water, stock or wine to cover the vegetables. Braising can be done on top of the cooker or in the oven, but the pan must have a tightly fitting lid to prevent loss of moisture. Meat should be braised in a slow oven, 180°C (350°F) mark 4, or over a low heat on top of the cooker, for 50 minutes per ½ kg (45 minutes per 1 lb). With a minimum of 2 hours for joints, 1½–2 hours for steaks and ¾–1 hour for chops.

After cooking, the meat is removed and the cooking liquor reduced by boiling, and used to glaze the meat. The vegetables can be served with the meat, but as they are very well cooked it is usually more satisfactory to liquidise them, and use them as a basis for a sauce or gravy. If the braise is chilled overnight, any fat can be skimmed off before reheating.

Pot roasting. This is really a combination of frying and steaming. The meat is browned all over, then covered and cooked slowly with a minimum amount of liquid either in the oven or on top of the cooker.

The joint should be turned every 30 minutes, but do not remove the lid at other times, or the steam will be released. Allow 50 minutes per ½ kg (45 minutes per 1 lb) in an oven at 180°C (350°F) mark 4.

Using a pressure cooker for the moist cooking methods will reduce the cooking time to a third, in most cases. Consult the manufacturer's instructions for details. The amount of liquid required is usually a third less.

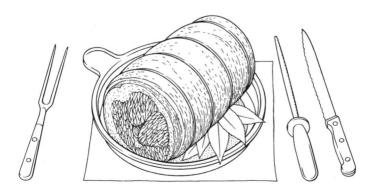

Cuts suitable for different cooking methods

Cooking method	Beef	Pork	Lamb

Frying & Grilling	Rump ⎫
	Fillet ⎬ Steaks
	Sirloin ⎭
		Fillet
		  (tenderloin)
		Loin chops
		Spare rib chops
		Belly – sliced
			Best end of
			  neck cutlets
			Loin ⎫
			Chump ⎬ Chops

Roasting	Topside
	Sirloin
	Fore rib
	Silverside
	Thick flank
		Neck end
		  (spare rib &
		  blade bone)
		Loin
		Leg
		Hand & spring
		Belly
			Loin
			Best end of
			  neck
			Leg
			Shoulder
			Breast

Braising	Chuck & blade Brisket Thin flank Thick flank Topside Silverside Thick rib	Spare rib chops Belly	Middle neck Breast Shoulder Scrag
Pot Roasting	Silverside Thick flank Topside Thick rib Thin rib Brisket		

Boiling	Brisket
	  (salted)
	Silverside
	  (salted)
		Belly (can be
		  salted)
		Hand & spring
		  (can be salted)	

Stewing	Thin flank Shin Leg Neck & clod Chuck & blade Skirt	Hand & spring Shoulder	Scrag Breast Middle neck

NB: All cuts of pork and most lamb cuts can be roasted.

Carving and serving

Carving is no problem given a few simple rules. The essential tools are a two pronged fork with a finger guard, a large sharp carving or cook's knife and an effective means of sharpening the knife at regular intervals. Boned and rolled joints are simply cut through. The butcher will usually bone a joint if asked, however with a good sharp knife and practice, it is easy to do yourself. Start from where the bone can be seen, work along it, cutting the meat away and follow the bone through. Any slips of the knife can be sewn up with cotton before cooking, provided it is removed before serving. Carving bone-in joints varies according to the position and shape of the bone. As a general rule, meat is carved down on to the bone, and the slice then cut off the bone.

Where a joint contains a backbone, chining by the butcher will aid carving. Ensure that the meat is stable, on a wooden board or spiked meat dish, which should be on a non-slip surface.

Wherever possible cut across the grain to shorten the muscle fibre length. When carving a leg or shoulder, it is often easier to hold the shank bone with one hand, using a tissue or paper towel. When doing this, the cutting edge of the knife must be angled away from the hand. With legs and shoulders, cut the meat down to the bone on one side and remove, then turn the joint over and repeat, or cut slices horizontally from the other side.

Inexperienced cooks may prefer to carve in the kitchen and reheat the meat to serve. Learning to carve can be a slow business, and the meat and vegetables can be cold by the time everything is ready. New cutting techniques and boneless joints, which are becoming more popular, will make carving and serving very much easier. Cold meat cuts up more economically than hot, and overcooked meat far less economically.

If meat is carved cold for reheating, it is imperative that the reheating must be quick and thorough, the meat must be served immediately and any not consumed discarded. All meat once cooked must be kept protected from contamination by dirt and pests, and refrigerated as quickly as possible. Warm meat is an ideal breeding ground for the bacteria that are responsible for food poisoning.

Accompaniments when serving meat

Meat	Sauces	Stuffing	Accompaniments
Beef	Horseradish cream / Horseradish in white sauce / Mustard sauce / Brown onion sauce / Red wine sauce	Sausage meat / Cooked rice and bacon / Mashed chestnuts / Chopped cooked celery / Mushroom and herbs	Yorkshire pudding / Batter popovers / Roast parsnips / Suet or oatmeal dumplings
Veal	Thick gravy, sherry-flavoured / Tomato sauce / Cumberland sauce / Sherry or Marsala sauce	Lemon and thyme / Cooked rice and ham / Chopped parsley and bacon (cooked) / Walnut orange and coriander	Bacon rolls / Baked ham or bacon / Risotto noodles or spaghetti
Lamb & Mutton	Mint sauce / Onion sauce / Caper sauce / Madeira sauce	Garlic, cooked rice and capers / Rosemary and/or onions / Mint or watercress / Lentil	Suet or oatmeal dumplings / Braised onions / Potato and onion casserole / Red currant or mint jelly
Pork	Thin gravy, cider-flavoured / Apple sauce / Gooseberry purée / Cranberry sauce or jelly	Sage and onion / Chopped apples and raisins / Chopped cooked celery and onions / Prunes and walnuts / Apricot and walnut	Pease pudding / Sauerkraut / Baked apples / Cucumber salad / Baked beans / Red cabbage / Apple cake

Meat	Sauces	Stuffing	Accompaniments
Bacon & Gammon	Parsley sauce	Prunes	Apple or
	Cumberland sauce	Sage and onion	pineapple rings
	Mustard sauce	Chopped apples and walnuts	Half peaches Butter beans in parsley
	Gravy with cider	Almond and raisin	sauce
	Clove and brown sugar coating	Apricot	Pease pudding
	Raisin sauce		

The table above gives some traditional accompaniments and new ideas. Some of the recipes appear in Stuffings and Accompaniments (see pages 86–93).

Measurements
The recipes in this book have been designed for either metric or imperial weights to be used. They should not be mixed.
Teaspoon refers to a 5 ml spoon, and tablespoon to a 15 ml spoon throughout.
Eggs are size 3 or 4.
Cooking times may vary slightly if cuts of meat are thicker or thinner than usual, or if thick pots and containers, requiring additional heating, are used.

American equivalents

	Metric	Imperial	American
Butter, margarine	225 g	8 oz	1 cup
Flour	100 g	4 oz	1 cup
Breadcrumbs, fresh	75 g	3 oz	1¾ cups
Cheese, grated	100 g	4 oz	1¼ cups

An American pint is 16 fl oz compared with the imperial pint of 20 fl oz. A standard American cup measure is considered to hold 8 fl oz.

BEEF AND VEAL

An interesting selection of beef and veal
recipes ranging from Pot Roast Beef with
Whisky to Veal Orloff – to suit every
taste and budget

Beef

When buying beef, it will be bright red when it is first cut, but goes darker on exposure to air. Look for fine even graining and firm fat. The colour of the fat depends on the breed and its feed, but is usually creamy white. Avoid meat which is dried or discoloured, and if it has too much marbling fat within the lean.

Principal cuts of beef In some areas regional names may be found.

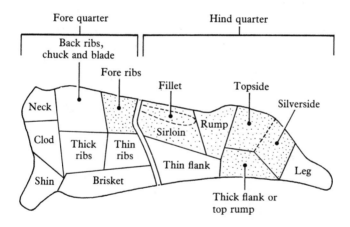

The shaded areas show cuts with small amounts of gristle which are suitable for roasting, grilling and frying (the dry methods).

Unshaded areas have more gristle and need to be cooked by a moist method (stewing, casseroling and braising) to make the meat tender.

Cuts of beef

Shin (foreleg) and leg (hindleg). This is lean meat with a high proportion of gristle. It requires long slow moist cooking and can be used for stews, casseroles, stocks, soup and brawn.

Neck and clod. Normally cut up as stewing steak or minced.

Chuck and blade steak. A large, fairly lean cut of meat, removed from the bone and sold as chuck steak for braising, stewing and pies.

Brisket. Brisket is sold in pieces, on the bone, or boned and rolled, and is suitable for braising or boiling. It can be salted and is excellent boiled and served cold. It is recognised by its layers of fat and lean.

Thin and thick ribs. These are usually sold boned and rolled, for braising or pot roasting.

Fore ribs. A good roasting joint on the bone or boned and rolled. This is the traditional cut for 'Roast beef of old England'.

Sirloin. A tender and delicious cut of meat from the loin. It is sold either on or off the bone as a joint for roasting, or as steaks for grilling or frying. Sirloin steaks are slices of the main back muscle, sometimes called the eye muscle, removed from the backbone, but still with its layer of back fat. T-bone steaks are the same cut, but cut through the T-shaped backbone, and include a piece of the fillet muscle as well. Porterhouse steaks are cut from the fore rib end.

Fillet steak. The fillet is a long muscle running along the inside of the backbone, in the sirloin area. It is very tender as the muscle is hardly used in the live animal, consequently it is much sought after and therefore very expensive. Although tender, it often does not have as much flavour as other cuts of beef. It is sold whole, or in large pieces for such classic dishes as Beef Wellington (fillet steak in a puff pastry case) or in slices as fillet steak. It can be tied to keep it round, and steaks cut from this are called tournedos. Cut into strips, it is the basis for Beef Stroganoff, and minced, for Steak Tartare. The Châteaubriand steak is cut from the place where the fillet divides to join the muscles of the rump.

Rump steak. This is an excellent lean and tender cut,

usually sold in slices for grilling and frying. Steaks
are cut down, through the back fat to the hip bone,
and have a characteristic, oblong shape, with the fat
at one end. One slice of rump steak, depending on
the area from which it comes, is often enough to
serve two.

Thin flank. Ideal for braising or stewing, it is often
salted or pickled, and frequently sold as mince.

Thick flank. A lean cut suitable for roasting, pot
roasting and braising, or when sliced for braising or
frying.

Topside. A lean cut, with little or no naturally occur-
ring fat, it is usually sold in rolled joints, which have
had a layer of fat tied round them. It roasts and pot
roasts well.

Silverside. A very lean joint, often treated like topside. If roasting, baste while cooking to prevent drying out. Silverside is traditionally salted and sold for
boiling, and is used for boiled beef and carrots.
Uncooked salted beef is grey, but turns its characteristic pink during cooking.

Veal

The cuts of veal correspond in name and position
with those of lamb (see page 38). However, the shank
end of the leg is more usually called the knuckle end
and the fillet end is often cut in thin slices, which are
beaten out to produce escalopes. The animal is larger
than the lamb, so joints, chops etc are correspond-
ingly bigger. Cuts can be cooked in the same way, the
lower part of the legs and necks are best stewed, the
remainder can be roasted, grilled or fried according
to cut. Take care if the veal is very thin that it does
not dry out during cooking. Cover with a sauce, foil
or a lid if necessary. Veal cooks very quickly, and
spoils if overcooked. Marinading will often add
flavour, and help to keep the meat moist during
cooking.

BEEF CARBONNADE

Serves 4

450–700 g (1–1½ lb) chuck steak in
  large cubes
1 tbsp flour
2 tbsp oil
seasoning
1 large onion, sliced
4 celery stalks, chopped
2 carrots, sliced
275 ml (½ pint) beer or stout
1 tbsp vinegar
1 bouquet garni
1 tbsp chopped parsley to garnish

Heat the oven to 170°C (325°F) mark 3 or
simmer the carbonnade on top of the stove.
Toss the meat in the flour and then fry in oil
to brown. Season to taste and add the onion,
celery and carrots and fry for a few minutes.
Add the beer, vinegar and bouquet garni.
Stir well and transfer to a warm casserole
with lid, or cook on a very low heat in a
covered pan.

Cook for 2–2½ hours or until the meat is
tender. Add a little water to the casserole if
it becomes dry during cooking. Discard
bouquet garni and adjust seasoning.
Garnish with chopped parsley.

Serve with creamed or jacket potatoes.

STEAK, KIDNEY AND MUSHROOM PIE

Serves 4–6

225 g (8 oz) flaky or mixer pastry
  using plain flour (see pages
  92–93)
450 g (1 lb) stewing steak in 2.5 cm
  (1 in) cubes
100–225 g (4–8 oz) young ox
  kidney
1 tbsp flour, seasoned
½ tsp mixed herbs
1 onion, finely chopped or left whole
  and spiked with cloves
100 g (4 oz) mushrooms, sliced
water or stock
egg for glazing

If time is short, the filling can be cooked in a
pressure cooker, as for a stew, but for the
best flavour, and most delicious pie, the
meat should be cooked from raw, under the
pastry crust.

Heat the oven to 220°C (425°F) mark 7
for flaky and 200°C (400°F) mark 6 for
mixer pastry.

Make the pastry and leave in a cool place
to relax. Toss the steak and kidney in
seasoned flour. Mix in the herbs, onion and
mushrooms. Place in a 1 litre (2 pint) pie
dish (with a flat rim). Ensure the dish is full,
if necessary pad out with raw potato. Add
sufficient stock or water to come half way
up the meat.

Roll out the pastry to the shape of dish
plus about 1 cm (½ in) extra all round. Cut
out the shape of the pie dish. Use the
trimmings to cover the rim of pie dish. Use

water to stick the pastry to the dish. Cover with pastry, pressing down the edges to seal. Knock up the edges, making horizontal cuts with the back of a small knife, then flute around rim of pie by bringing up the back of a knife, every 5 cm (2 in). Decorate with pastry leaves, and cut a hole in the middle to release the steam. Glaze with beaten egg. Bake for 30 minutes, then reduce heat to 180°C (350°F) mark 4 for a further 1½–2 hours until meat feels tender when tried with a skewer through the hole in the top. If necessary cover pastry with greaseproof paper to prevent burning. Top up with stock if required.
Serve with extra gravy.

PEPPERED BEEF

Serves 4

25 g (1 oz) flour
1 tsp ground ginger
seasoning
450–700 g (1–1½ lb) braising steak
3 tbsp oil
225 g (8 oz) tomatoes, skinned
1–2 tsp chilli or Tabasco sauce
1 tbsp Worcester sauce
2 tbsp wine vinegar
2 cloves garlic, crushed
150 ml (¼ pint) tomato juice or stock
1 small red pepper, decored, in rings
1 small green pepper, decored, in rings
1 yellow pepper, decored, in rings (if available)
100 g (4 oz) mushrooms

Heat the oven to 170°C (325°F) mark 3. Mix the flour, ginger and seasoning and rub into the steak. Fry in the oil to brown both sides. Transfer to a casserole dish.

In a liquidiser, combine the tomatoes, chilli sauce, Worcester sauce, vinegar, garlic and tomato juice. Pour over meat, cover and cook for about 1½ hours. Add the peppers and mushrooms and cook for a further 30 minutes or until meat is tender and pepper cooked but not too soft.

A can of red kidney beans can be added with the peppers if desired. This will stretch the meal to serve 6, and provide vegetable protein and fibre.

Serve with rice, pasta or jacket potatoes.

BEEF STROGANOFF

Serves 4

450–700 g (1–1½ lb) fillet steak in
  thin strips
ground black pepper
½ tsp basil
25 g (1 oz) butter
1 tbsp oil
50 g (2 oz) streaky bacon in strips
1 onion, finely chopped
225 g (8 oz) mushrooms, sliced
½ tsp ground mace
1 tbsp parsley, chopped
150–275 ml (¼–½ pint) soured
  cream or natural yoghurt
chopped parsley to garnish

Season the steak with the pepper and basil.
Heat the butter and oil and stir fry the steak
and bacon for about 5 minutes until the
meat is browned all over. Remove the meat
from pan and keep warm. Add the onion to
the pan and fry gently until transparent;
add the mushrooms and fry for 3 minutes.
Return the meat to pan and add the mace,
parsley and cream. Heat through but do not
boil.

Serve garnished with parsley on a bed of
boiled rice.

GOULASH WITH NATURAL YOGHURT

Serves 4

450–700 g (1–1½ lb) stewing beef
  (or veal) in 2.5 cm (1 in) cubes
3 tbsp oil
1 large onion, chopped
1 clove garlic, finely chopped
2 tbsp paprika
½ tsp caraway seeds
400 g (14 oz) can of tomatoes
425 ml (¾ pint) beef stock
1 red pepper, deseeded and cut in
  strips
450 g (1 lb) potatoes, scrubbed and
  sliced
100 g (4 oz) button mushrooms
black pepper to taste
150 ml (¼ pint) natural yoghurt (or
  soured cream)

Heat the oven to 150°C (300°F) mark 2 or
simmer on top of the stove in a pan. Brown
the meat in hot oil. Add the onion, garlic,
paprika and caraway seeds and fry for a few
minutes, stirring continuously. Add the
tomatoes and stock. Cook with a lid on, for
2–3 hours until meat is tender.

Add the pepper and potatoes for the last
45 minutes, and the mushrooms for the last
10 minutes. Adjust the seasoning, serve in a
heated dish, with yoghurt poured on top,
and swirled in.

Serve with a green or mixed salad. The
potatoes can be omitted and the goulash
served with dumplings, pasta or rice.

POT ROAST BEEF WITH WHISKY

Serves 4–6

900 g (2 lb) joint (flank, top rib or
  chuck)
4 tbsp oil
2 carrots, sliced
2 small parsnips, sliced
1 stick of celery, chopped
75 ml (3 fl oz) whisky

Heat the oven to 180°C (350°F) mark 4. If possible, use a casserole in which the meat can be fried and roasted, or use a frying pan and then transfer the meat and fat to an earthenware casserole to pot roast.

Brown the joint well in oil. Add the vegetables around the joint and pour in the whisky. Cover with a well-fitting lid. Cook for about 2 hours, turning the joint once, until the meat is tender. Remove the meat to a heated serving dish. Use the cooking liquor, liquidised if preferred, diluted with water and suitably thickened, for a sauce or gravy.

BEEF SLICES IN RED WINE

Serves 4

4 slices of topside or similar, about
  1 cm (½ in) thick
150 ml (¼ pint) red wine
1 onion, finely chopped
1 bay leaf
1 tsp parsley
¼ tsp marjoram
¼ tsp thyme
25 g (1 oz) flour
3 tbsp oil
275 ml (½ pint) beef stock
seasoning to taste
225 g (8 oz) button onions
225 g (8 oz) baby carrots
2 tbsp chopped parsley to garnish

Lay the meat in shallow dish, or in sealable polythene container. Pour over the wine, add the onion and herbs and marinade for several hours but preferably overnight.

Heat the oven to 150°C (300°F) mark 2. Drain the meat well, reserving marinade. Coat with flour and fry in oil to brown. Place meat in a casserole dish. Add any remaining flour to the fat, and cook to brown, but do not burn.

Slowly add the stock and marinade. Season to taste, and pour over meat. Cover and cook slowly for 1–1½ hours. Add onions and carrots and cook for a further hour until meat is tender.

Serve sprinkled with chopped parsley.

Other meats can be cooked in this way, using white wine with lighter meats.

SLICED BEEF IN ASPIC

Serves 4

8 slices rare roast beef
cooked carrot, sliced
cooked button onions
fresh herb leaves

Aspic
425 ml (¾ pint) well flavoured stock
150 ml (¼ pint) Madeira wine
1 pkt or 4 tsp gelatine
1 tsp Worcester sauce
pinch cayenne pepper

Place the meat in a shallow serving dish and arrange in overlapping slices. Decorate by placing the carrot and onions between the slices. Arrange the herb leaves on top.

Heat the stock and Madeira. Sprinkle on gelatine and leave to dissolve. Add Worcester sauce and cayenne pepper. Cool until aspic is syrupy. Glaze the beef and chill. Place the remaining aspic in a shallow dish and, when set, cut into cubes. Use chopped aspic to decorate the meat by forming two rows on either side of it.

Serve with a salad or as part of a buffet table.

BEEF AND HARICOT BEANS

Serves 4

100 g (4 oz) haricot beans, soaked
    overnight
450 g (1 lb) chuck or braising steak
    in 2.5 cm (1 in) cubes
100 g (4 oz) lean streaky bacon
    pieces
1 large onion, sliced
2 carrots, sliced
2 cloves garlic, crushed
225 g (8 oz) tomatoes, skinned
bouquet garni or 1 tsp herbs
275 ml (½ pint) stock
275 ml (½ pint) red wine or further
    stock
seasoning to taste
chopped parsley to garnish

Put all ingredients into a large pan and bring to the boil. Stir well and cover with a well fitting lid. Simmer for 2–2½ hours until meat is tender.

The casserole should not need thickening as the haricot beans will absorb excess liquid, but adjust consistency if necessary.

Serve sprinkled with chopped parsley.

This dish reheats well next day, and is delicious served with a chunk of granary bread.

BEEF AND PRUNE RAGOUT

Serves 4

575 ml (1 pint) beef stock, beer or
   wine
225 g (8 oz) prunes
450–700 g (1–1½ lb) chuck steak in
   cubes or pieces
25 g (1 oz) seasoned flour
3 tbsp oil
1 tbsp tomato purée
2 bay leaves
225 g (8 oz) small tomatoes, skinned

Heat the stock and pour over the prunes.
Leave to soak, if possible overnight. Coat
the meat in flour and fry in oil to brown.
Add the tomato purée, bay leaves and about
6 finely chopped prunes, with the drained
stock. Simmer for 1¾ hours, until meat is
tender. Add the remaining prunes and
tomatoes, whole, and cook for
approximately 20 minutes until the prunes
are soft but prunes and tomatoes have not
collapsed in shape.
   Serve with potatoes, pasta or rice.
   Prunes can be replaced with dried
apricots, peaches or large raisins.

BOILED SALT BEEF

Serves 6–8

900 g (2 lb) salt brisket
cold beef stock to cover
2 onions, quartered
4 carrots, sliced
1 small turnip, chopped
1 tsp black peppercorns
2 tsp mixed herbs

Soak the brisket overnight, then drain and
discard soaking water. Place the meat in a
large pan and cover with stock. Add the
vegetables and seasonings (do not add salt).
Cover and bring to the boil. Simmer, very
slowly for about 1½ hours.
   Served sliced with unthickened cooking
liquor and vegetables, and boiled potatoes.
If serving cold, allow to cool in cooking
liquor, slice and serve with salads or in
sandwiches, with horseradish sauce.

STIR FRY BEEF

Serves 4–6

1 tbsp cornflour
450 g (1 lb) rump steak in paper thin
    slices
3 tbsp oil
4 spring onions, finely chopped
100–175 g (4–6 oz) Chinese leaves
    or white cabbage, finely shredded
75 g (3 oz) bean sprouts
2 sticks celery, finely chopped
1 tbsp soy sauce or more to taste

Mix the cornflour to a paste with 3 tbsp water and mix with steak. Heat the oil and stir fry the meat for about 3 minutes, over a high heat in a frying pan or wok. Remove from the pan, drain and keep hot.

Adding a little more oil if necessary, stir fry the vegetables, also over a high heat, for about 5 minutes or until cooked to taste. The vegetables should still be crisp. Pour over soy sauce, return the meat to the pan and stir well.

Serve immediately with boiled or fried rice, or as part of a Chinese meal.

CARPET BAG STEAKS

Serves 4

4 thick pieces of fillet or rump steak
24 prepared mussels (or 12 oysters),
    fresh, canned, frozen or smoked
50 g (2 oz) butter
2 tbsp parsley, chopped
1 clove garlic, crushed
2 tbsp lemon juice
seasoning
melted butter
ground black pepper

Split the steaks to make pockets. Mix the mussels with butter, parsley, garlic, lemon and seasoning, and divide between the pockets in the steaks. Skewer or sew up. Brush with melted butter and sprinkle with ground black pepper.

Grill or fry until cooked to personal taste. The cooking time will depend on thickness of the steak and the heat of the grill or pan. Turn once during cooking, and serve immediately with tomatoes, mushrooms and potatoes.

SWISS STEAKS

Serves 4

1 tbsp seasoned flour
4 × 1 cm (½ in) thick slices of
   topside or similar
25 g (1 oz) butter or margarine
1 large onion, finely chopped
2 sticks celery, finely chopped
400 g (14 oz) can tomatoes, broken
   up
2 tsp tomato purée
½ tsp Worcester sauce
150 ml (¼ pint) stock or water
4 tbsp single cream or yoghurt
   (optional)

Press flour well into slices of meat. Fry in butter to brown both sides. Add the onion and cook for a few minutes. Stir in celery, tomatoes, purée, Worcester sauce and stock, cover and simmer, or put into a casserole dish, and cook covered at 170°C (325°F) mark 3 for 2–2½ hours until meat is tender.

Serve topped with cream or yoghurt, with boiled or creamed potatoes and fresh green vegetables.

STEAK DIANE

Serves 4

450 g (1 lb) grilling or frying steak
   beaten out to ½ cm (¼ in) thick
25 g (1 oz) butter
3 tbsp oil
1 onion, very finely chopped
1 clove garlic, crushed
50 g (2 oz) bacon, finely chopped
100 g (4 oz) mushrooms, finely
   chopped
1 tbsp fresh chives, chopped
freshly ground black pepper
3 tbsp brandy, warmed
150 ml (¼ pint) single cream

Cut the beaten steak into approximately 7.5 cm (3 in) square. Heat some of the butter and oil and when hot, fry the steak for 1½ minutes on either side. Drain and keep warm. Adding more fat if required, fry the onion for 2 minutes, add the garlic, bacon, mushrooms, chives and seasoning, and stir fry to cook, approximately 3 minutes. Return the meat to the pan.

Warm the brandy, pour over meat and ignite. Let the brandy burn until it extinguishes. Pour in the cream and warm but do not boil.

Serve on a warm platter with potato piped around as a border. This dish can be garnished with bacon rolls, sliced mushrooms or chopped parsley.

BEEF STEAK EN CROUTE

Serves 4–6

marinade (optional, see page 91)
4 fillet steaks or a piece 1–1½ kg
   (2–3 lb)
225 g (8 oz) flaky or mixer pastry
   using plain flour (see pages 92 and
   93)
1 onion, finely chopped
oil for frying, with some butter if
   preferred
100 g (4 oz) mushrooms, finely
   chopped
100 g (4 oz) liver pâté
2 tbsp brandy
3 tbsp cream
freshly ground black pepper
egg to glaze

If using the marinade, steep meat in it for a few hours, or overnight. Drain. The marinade can be used as a basis for a sauce.

Make the pastry and leave in the refrigerator to relax. Fry the onion in oil until soft, add the mushrooms and cook for a few minutes. Mix onions, mushrooms, pâté, brandy and cream together.

Heat the oil and butter and fry steaks for 1 minute each side. If using a large piece of meat, fry turning regularly to brown, for about 5 minutes. Longer or shorter cooking at this stage will make the finished steak more well done or rarer.

If using a large piece of meat, slit down but not through, into portions. Spread pâté mixture on each steak, or in the slits of the larger piece. Sprinkle well with freshly ground black pepper. Heat the oven to 230°C (450°F) mark 8.

Roll the pastry out into 4 circles, or an oblong approximately 20 × 25 cm (8 × 10 in), trim the edges. Place the fillets pâté side down on the pastry, dampen edges with water, and make into a parcel; wrap the pastry around the large piece. Place on baking tray, join side down. Decorate with pastry leaves made from trimmings, and glaze with beaten egg. Bake in a hot oven for 20–25 minutes for individual, and 40–45 minutes for a large croûte. The pastry should be well risen and golden brown.

Serve immediately.

Variations
Use ham or bacon, or chopped anchovies in place of the pâté.
The piece of steak can be prepared as above, and then roasted for 45–60 minutes and served without being cooked en croute.

POTTED MEAT

Serves 4–6

225 g (8 oz) shin of beef in small cubes
1 knuckle end of veal (pork if veal unavailable)
½ tsp salt
6 allspice berries
6 peppercorns
1 onion, whole
1 bay leaf

Put all ingredients in a lidded pan with enough water to cover, simmer slowly for 2–3 hours until meat falls away from the bones.
Remove the meat from cooking liquor and take out the bones. Shred the meat using a knife and fork and place in an oiled mould. Reduce cooking liquor to about 275 ml (½ pint) and strain over meat. Leave to set.
Turn out and cut in slices for serving with salads or in sandwiches.

BRAISED BEEF AND CHESTNUTS

Serves 4

marinade (optional, see page 91) or 275 ml (½ pint) stock, if not using marinade
450–700 g (1–1½ lb) lean braising steak, cut 2.5 cm (1 in) thick
450 g (1 lb) mixed vegetables in season in 1 cm (½ in) cubes
100 g (4 oz) dried or 225 g (8 oz) fresh, cooked chestnuts
1 red pepper, decored and sliced
150 ml (¼ pint) beef stock

If using marinade, steep meat in it for several hours, but preferably overnight. Heat the oven to 170°C (325°F) mark 3. Place vegetables in casserole dish with dried chestnuts. Place meat on top. Pour over stock or marinade. Cover and cook slowly for 1½–2 hours. Add pepper 30 minutes from the end of cooking, with fresh chestnuts if used. If the lid is not tightly fitting, more stock may be required.
Serve with jacket potatoes cooked at the same time.

BRAISED MARINADED BEEF

Serves 4–8

marinade (see page 91)
1–2 kg (2–4 lb) joint of beef
  (brisket, chuck, top ribs)
4 tbsp oil
50 g (2 oz) streaky bacon pieces
225 g (8 oz) onions, quartered
225 g (8 oz) carrots in strips
seasoning to taste
stock or water

Marinade the meat for several hours, but preferably overnight. If using the oven, heat to 180°C (350°F) mark 4.

Use a deep pan or enamelled casserole and brown the joint of meat well in the oil. Remove meat. Add the bacon, vegetables, and seasoning, fry to brown. Leave in pan or transfer to casserole dish if necessary. Place meat on top.

Make the marinade up to 275 ml (½ pint) with stock or water and pour onto meat. Cover and simmer or cook in oven for 2½–3 hours until the meat is cooked. Turn the joint over once during cooking.

Serve on a bed of boiled noodles with the vegetables around, or liquidised and used as a basis for a gravy or sauce.

VEAL GALANTINE

Serves 8–12

1.5 kg (3 lb) breast of veal in one
  piece
450 g (1 lb) good quality sausage
  meat
225 g (8 oz) gammon or bacon in
  small cubes
3 hard-boiled eggs, whole or sliced
1 onion, whole
¼ tsp thyme
¼ tsp parsley
1 bay leaf
1 level tbsp powdered gelatine

Bone out the veal and keep the bones. Lay breast, skin side down, out flat. Spread the sausage meat and chopped gammon evenly over the veal. Add the eggs, either as a line down the middle, or as a layer of sliced egg over the meats. Roll up and sew together with cotton, leaving the end hanging free. Wrap firmly in foil, or greaseproof paper and pudding cloth.

Place the bones in a large pan with the onion and herbs. Place the galantine on top. Cover with water. Bring to the boil and then simmer for 2–3 hours, until tender. Using a pressure cooker reduces this time to 1 hour. Remove the galantine and press it between two plates until cold. Reduce the cooking liquor to 275 ml (½ pint) by boiling rapidly. Strain, discarding bones.

Sprinkle the gelatine on to the reduced liquor and stir to dissolve. Use on the point of setting, to glaze galantine, which can be left whole, or carved into overlapping slices. Serve as a buffet with various salads, or for a picnic, or packed lunch.

VEAL MILANESE

Serves 4

4 escalopes, well beaten, or veal steaks
seasoned flour to coat
1 beaten egg
breadcrumbs
oil for frying

Sauce
1 onion, grated
2 tbsp oil
3–4 tbsp tomato purée
1 tsp sugar
15 g (½ oz) flour
275 ml (½ pint) stock

To serve
225 g (8 oz) pasta shapes
15 g (½ oz) butter
25 g (1 oz) grated Parmesan cheese

Dredge the meat in seasoned flour, pat well in, then coat with the egg and breadcrumbs.

Make the sauce by tossing grated onion in hot oil and cooking for 1 minute. Stir in the tomato purée, sugar and flour and cook for a few minutes. Slowly add stock and boil for 5 minutes to thicken and cook flour.

Boil the pasta in plenty of slightly salted water until it is tender but still firm, about 12 minutes for white pasta, and 15–17 minutes for wholemeal. While the pasta is cooking, fry the prepared meat in oil until cooked, and golden brown, about 3 minutes a side for very thin escalopes up to 10 minutes a side for thick steaks. When cooked, drain well and keep hot. Drain the pasta and stir in melted butter.

Serve cooked meat, overlapping, on a bed of buttered pasta, with the tomato sauce poured over, and Parmesan cheese sprinkled on top.

CHINESE VEAL

Serves 4–8

1 tbsp cornflour
1 tsp ground ginger
seasoning to taste
450 g (1 lb) veal (or beef), well
  beaten and cut in strips
4 tbsp oil
1 onion, sliced
150 ml (¼ pint) light stock or water
1 tbsp soy sauce
1 tbsp sherry
½ red pepper, deseeded and in strips
50 g (2 oz) mushrooms, sliced
1 tbsp crystallised ginger, chopped
15 g (½ oz) cornflour

Mix the cornflour and ginger with the seasoning and coat meat strips well. Shallow fry in oil (or deep fat fry if preferred), stirring to prevent burning, until meat is cooked, about 7–10 minutes. Drain and keep warm.

Place the onion in a pan with the stock, soy sauce and sherry, and boil for 3–5 minutes. Add the pepper and cook for a further 2–3 minutes and add the mushrooms and cook for 1–2 more minutes. Stir in ginger. Vegetables should still be crisp. Blend the cornflour with a little water and use to thicken vegetable mixture.

Serve in a hot bowl, with fried meat added on top at the last minute. Vegetables can be cooked at the same time as the meat, but do not let vegetables stand or they will get soft.

Serve with boiled rice, or as part of a Chinese meal.

ORANGE TARRAGON VEAL

Serves 4

4 veal chops or shoulder steaks
1 tbsp flour, seasoned
15 g (½ oz) butter
2 tbsp oil
1 large onion, sliced
175 g (6 oz) concentrated orange
  juice (usually frozen)
150 ml (¼ pint) chicken stock
1 tbsp dried tarragon leaves
15 g (½ oz) cornflour
150 ml (¼ pint) soured cream or
  natural yoghurt

Heat the oven to 180°C (350°F) mark 4 or simmer on top of the stove in a pan. Coat the meat in seasoned flour. Heat the butter and oil together and fry the meat to brown on both sides. Stir in the onion and fry for a few minutes. Add the orange juice and stock (if concentrated juice cannot be obtained, use 325 ml (12 fl oz) normal strength, and dissolve a stock cube in it instead of using stock). Stir in tarragon and simmer or cook in oven for 1–1½ hours until meat is tender.

Place the meat in a hot serving dish and keep warm. Thicken cooking liquor with cornflour to give a coating consistency. Stir in the soured cream and heat but do not boil. Pour over meat.

The dish can be garnished with fresh tarragon, orange slices or orange rind julienne strips.

VEAL VERONIQUE

Serves 4

4 veal (or pork) escalopes or chops, deboned
small onion, finely chopped
50 g (2 oz) mushrooms, finely chopped
40 g (1½ oz) butter
½ tsp herbs to taste
seasoning to taste
75 ml (⅛ pint) white wine
75 ml (⅛ pint) stock
150 ml (¼ pint) milk
25 g (1 oz) cornflour
100 g (4 oz) white grapes, skinned and deseeded

Heat the oven to 190°C (375°F) mark 5 or cook on top of stove. Beat the escalopes to 1 cm (½ in) thick or trim the chops and make a pocket slit with a sharp knife. Fry the onion and mushrooms in 15 g (½ oz) of butter until cooked. Either spread the onion and mushroom mixture on the escalopes, roll up and secure with a cocktail stick, or push the mixture into the slits in the chops. Place in a casserole or pan with herbs, seasoning, wine and stock and cook slowly either in the oven or in a saucepan for 1–1½ hours until the meat is tender.

Remove the meat to a hot serving dish and keep warm. Strain the liquor and make up to 275 ml (½ pint) with milk. Heat the remaining butter and cornflour together and cook for 2–3 minutes. Gradually blend in the milk and cooking liquor and bring to the boil. Boil for 3–5 minutes until sauce is thick and glossy. Pour over meat and sprinkle grapes over the top. Return to the oven for a few minutes if necessary, to heat through.

The dish can be garnished with boiled, sieved, or piped potatoes.

VEAL AND BEAN RAGOUT

Serves 4

450–700 g (1–1½ lb) stewing veal
  (allow extra for bone)
2 tbsp oil
1 large onion, chopped
1 tbsp wholemeal flour, seasoned
½ tsp oregano
½ tsp grated nutmeg
225 g (8 oz) tomatoes, skinned and
  quartered
275 ml (½ pint) stock or wine and
  stock
225 g (8 oz) haricot or other beans,
  soaked overnight
chopped parsley to garnish

Brown the meat in the oil. Stir in the onion and cook for a few minutes. Stir in flour, oregano, nutmeg and tomatoes. Blend in the stock and wine, add the beans. Cover and simmer for 1½–2 hours until the meat is tender.

Garnish with chopped parsley and serve with boiled or baked potatoes in their jackets and fresh green vegetables.

VEAL AND HAM PIE

Serves 4–6

225 g (8 oz) flaky or mixer pastry
  (see pages 92–93)
450 g (1 lb) boneless veal in small
  cubes
175 g (6 oz) bacon, diced or pieces
2 hard-boiled eggs, sliced
1 tbsp parsley, chopped
1 tsp grated lemon rind
seasoning to taste
150 ml (¼ pint) stock, water or
  white wine
egg to glaze

Heat the oven to 230°C (450°F) mark 8. Roll out the pastry to the shape of the pie dish plus 1 cm (½ in) all round (use 1 litre (2 pint) size). Layer the veal, bacon, egg, parsley and lemon rind in pie dish and season. Add enough stock to come half way up the mixture.

To cover the pie, cut the pastry to the shape of the pie dish, and use 1 cm (½ in) trimming to make a ledge of pastry round the rim of the pie dish. Moisten this edge, and place on cut pastry shape. Press two layers together, knock up the edges with a small knife, and use the back of knife to flute round rim of pie, bringing it up every 4 cm (1½ in). Make a hole in the centre to allow the steam to escape. Use any trimmings to make leaves and rose for centre.

Glaze with beaten egg. Place on a baking tray and bake for 15 minutes, then turn down heat to 190°C (375°F) mark 5 for a further 1½ hours or until meat is tender when tested with a skewer through the hole in the top of the pie. If pastry is getting too brown, cover with greaseproof paper.

Serve hot with fresh vegetables, or cold with salad. If serving cold, stock can be topped up through the hole in the top, using veal bone stock, which will give a good set. For a picnic, use pastry below and above the meat, in order to cut out a good slice (double the quantity of pastry).

BLANQUETTE OF VEAL

Serves 4

450–700 g (1–1½ lb) shoulder or
   knuckle veal, cubed
225 g (8 oz) small onions
2 carrots, sliced
2 bay leaves
1 lemon, rind and juice
seasoning to taste
100 g (4 oz) button mushrooms
40 g (1½ oz) butter or margarine
40 g (1½ oz) flour or cornflour
1 egg yolk
150 ml (¼ pint) single cream or
   natural yoghurt
grated nutmeg

Put veal in a pan, cover with water and bring to the boil. Strain and rinse scum off veal.

Replace the veal in the pan with onions, carrots, bay leaves, lemon rind and juice and seasoning. Add 850 ml (1½ pints) water (or very light stock could be used), bring to the boil, cover and simmer for 1½ hours, adding mushrooms for last 30 minutes. Strain meat and vegetables and place on a warm serving dish, cover with foil and keep warm. Reduce cooking liquor to 575 ml (1 pint) by boiling rapidly.

Heat the butter and flour together to make a white roux. Cook for a few minutes, but do not allow to brown. Slowly blend cooking liquor into roux and heat and then boil for 5 minutes. Adjust seasoning as required. (If sauce is not smooth, strain or liquidise).

Beat in egg yolk and cream and heat but do not boil. Pour sauce over meat, and sprinkle with grated nutmeg.

VEAL OLIVES OR BIRDS

Serves 4

stuffing or forcemeat (1 quantity, see pages 87–89)
4 veal (or pork or beef) escalopes, well beaten out
1 tbsp flour
15 g (½ oz) butter or 2 tbsp oil
150 ml (¼ pint) chicken stock
150 ml (¼ pint) dry white wine (red if using beef)
bouquet garni
seasoning to taste
beurre manié (see page 90) or cornflour
75–150 ml (⅛–¼ pint) single cream or natural yoghurt
chopped parsley to garnish

Spread the stuffing evenly on the escalopes. Roll up and skewer or tie. Roll in the flour to coat and fry in butter to brown. Add the stock and wine and bring to the boil, stirring continuously. Lower heat to simmer, add the bouquet garni and seasoning and cook slowly for 45–60 minutes or until meat is tender when pierced with a skewer. Remove the skewers or string and the bouquet garni. Place veal olives in serving dish and keep warm.

Thicken the sauce to coating consistency using beurre manié or cornflour. Stir in cream and heat but do not boil. Coat the meat with the sauce, and serve garnished with chopped parsley. Potato can be piped around the dish, or served as duchesse potatoes.

OSSO BUCCO

Serves 4

4 thick slices shin of veal with plenty of meat on
1 tbsp flour with seasoning
2 tbsp olive oil
2 cloves garlic, finely chopped
1 Spanish onion, sliced
150 ml (¼ pint) light stock
150 ml (¼ pint) white wine or more stock
3 tbsp tomato purée
4 anchovy fillets, finely chopped
4 tbsp chopped parsley
grated rind ½ lemon

To serve
225 g (8 oz) long grain rice
pinch of saffron or ¼ tsp turmeric

Dredge the meat with seasoned flour and fry in oil to brown on both sides. Add the garlic, onion, stock, wine and tomato purée and bring to the boil. Cover and simmer for 1½–2 hours until meat is tender. Add the anchovy fillets and cook for 5 minutes.

Boil the rice with saffron or turmeric until cooked but not soft, about 12 minutes for white rice and 20 for brown. Drain, rinse and dry for 15 minutes.

Serve the Osso Bucco sprinkled with parsley and lemon rind, on a bed of, or with, the saffron rice.

VEAL ORLOFF

Serves 4–6

1–1½ kg (2–3 lb) boned, rolled and
  tied joint of veal or lamb
3 tbsp oil
2 onions, 1 quartered, 1 chopped
2 carrots, sliced
1 stick celery, chopped
bouquet garni
150 ml (¼ pint) stock or water
175 g (6 oz) mushrooms, chopped
15 g (½ oz) butter
seasoning to taste

Cheese sauce
25 g (1 oz) butter or margarine
25 g (1 oz) cornflour
275 ml (½ pint) milk
¼ tsp mustard
75 g (3 oz) grated cheese
1 tbsp breadcrumbs

Heat the oven to 200°C (400°F) mark 6. Fry the veal in oil to brown and transfer to a casserole dish. Add the quartered onion, carrot and celery with bouquet garni and stock. Cover and braise for 30 minutes. Lower the heat to 180°C (350°F) mark 4 and continue cooking for 1–1½ hours, until the meat juice runs clear when meat is pierced with a skewer.

Meanwhile fry the chopped onion and mushroom in the butter until soft and golden brown. Season as required.

Make the cheese sauce by heating the butter and cornflour together and cooking for 2–3 minutes. Slowly blend in milk and boil to thicken. Add the mustard, 50 g (2 oz) of the cheese and seasoning to taste. Stir to dissolve cheese.

Remove the meat from the braise and cut into 4 or 6 thick slices. Arrange on a serving dish with the mushroom and onion mix between slices. Coat with cheese sauce, sprinkle with 25 g (1 oz) grated cheese, and return to oven for 10–15 minutes to heat through and brown cheese.

This dish is fairly rich, so is best served with boiled rice or creamed potatoes and fresh, boiled vegetables.

The vegetables and liquor from the braise can be used as a basis for a gravy.

VEAL CORDON BLEU

Serves 4

*4 veal (or pork) escalopes beaten
    very thin
4 slices gruyère cheese (or Edam)
4 slices of ham
seasoning
beaten egg to coat
breadcrumbs to coat
lemon wedges and parsley to garnish*

This dish can be assembled in three ways. For thicker escalopes lay a cheese slice on a veal slice, top with a ham slice and season. Press well together and coat with egg and breadcrumbs. Shallow fat fry for 3–5 minutes a side depending on thickness of the meat.

For thin escalopes, lay a cheese then a ham slice on an escalope and season, roll up and skewer. Coat with egg and breadcrumbs and deep fat fry for about 10 minutes, until cooked through and golden brown.

For very thin escalopes, lay a cheese and ham slice on half of a veal slice and season. Fold over and sew round with cotton to enclose ham and cheese. Coat with egg and breadcrumbs. Shallow fat fry on medium heat for 5–7 minutes a side. Remove the cotton and serve.

For all methods, drain well and serve piled on a hot serving dish, garnished with lemon wedges and sprigs of parsley.

LAMB

A collection of recipes for every occasion from
Crown Roast of Lamb to delicious everyday
dishes such as Minted Lamb Parcels

British lamb is available fresh very nearly all the year round. It is cheapest and most plentiful from August until December. Britain imports frozen lamb from New Zealand. It is available all the year round, but has its 'new' season when British lamb is least available, from Christmas to Easter, when it can be a very economic buy.

When buying fresh lamb, look for firm, white fat, fine-grained, firm, pinky-brown lean, with very little gristle and a good proportion of lean to fat. Freshly cut surfaces should look slightly moist and the bones should be pinkish-blue.

Principal cuts of lamb In some areas regional names may be found

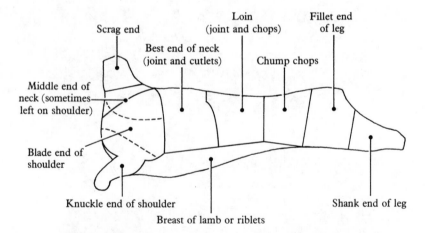

Cuts of lamb
Scrag and middle neck. These are usually sold chopped into pieces and are used for stewing and braising. They are traditionally used for Irish stew and Lancashire hot-pot. Increasingly the meat is being cut off the bone and sold as neck fillet, it is sweet and easy to cook, and very reasonably priced with no wastage.

On small animals and frozen carcases (such as New Zealand lamb) these cuts are left on the shoulder, and more often sold in two halves.

Shoulder. A succulent, sweet, tender roasting joint, whether on the bone, or boned and rolled, with or without stuffing. Shoulders are sold whole or halved into blade and knuckle ends, both ideal for roasting or braising. Frozen carcases are often cut into slices with a band-saw, giving shoulder steaks, weighing about 150 g (5 oz) each. These can be grilled, braised, baked or casseroled.

Best end of neck. This can be purchased as a roasting joint with 6–7 rib bones. If chined by the butcher, it is easier to carve. It can be roasted on the bone, or boned and rolled, with or without stuffing. It is frequently cut into cutlets with one rib bone to each. Two best ends of neck (preferably a pair from a left and right side) joined together and curved, bones outwards, makes a Crown Roast, and facing each other, fat side outwards, they make a Guard of Honour. Allow 2 cutlets per person. When boned and rolled and then cut into slices, the slices are known as noisettes.

Loin. This is either roasted in a piece, on the bone, or boned and rolled, with or without stuffing, or cut into chops for grilling, frying or braising. A loin will cut into 6–7 chops. Allow 1 or 2 chops per person according to appetite and money available. Occasionally, valentine chops or steaks can be found. These come from a boned loin, cut into 2.5 cm (1 in) slices, and each one is cut nearly through, from the fatty side, and opened out to give a heart shape. Occasionally double loin chops are found, these are cut across the animal before the two sides are separated down the backbone. If a whole double loin is cut out it is known as a saddle, which traditionally includes the kidneys at one end and has a plait and bow or rose made from strips of fat down the centre back. It is an excellent roast when serving 8–10 people. To carve a saddle, cut down either side of the back bone, flatten the knife to loosen meat from bone, then cut slices as if carving a single loin.

Chump. This can be sold as a piece, but is normally cut into chump chops. They are larger than loin chops and vary according to where along the chump they are from. Chump chops are distinguished by a small round bone in the centre. Some also have a large piece of backbone.

Leg. The prime joint, excellent for roasting or for cutting up into cubes of succulent tender meat. It can be cooked on the bone, or boned and rolled, with or without stuffing. It is frequently cut in two and sold as fillet and shank end. Slices off the fillet end are ideal for frying or grilling.

Breast. A long thin cut of lean, streaked with fat. Choose one with plenty of lean. This can be boned and rolled, which with a tasty stuffing, provides an economical roast or braise. Cut into strips it can be roast or barbecued, this cut is known as riblets. If casseroling or stewing it is sometimes worth roasting for 15 minutes to remove some of the fat, or boiling and discarding the water.

Boneless cutting methods. Many traditional roasting cuts, sold on the bone are impractical for small families, and those wanting a quick meal with no left overs for the next day. New techniques have been developed whereby the carcase can be boned, the resulting meat butchered and cut into small boneless joints, steaks and slices which are suitable for quick cooking methods such as frying and grilling. Excess fat can be removed and the meat cut into suitably sized joints for the customer's needs. These are not likely to replace the traditional joints for those who still want them, but do make the animal more versatile.

NOISETTES WITH RED CURRANT

Serves 4

marinade (optional, see page 92)
4–8 noisettes, chops or cutlets
red currant jelly
slices of wholemeal bread for croûtes
150 ml (¼ pint) stock
watercress to garnish

Marinade the meat overnight if required. Heat grill on high. Place the meat on the grid of the grill pan, ensuring pan is clean. Place 1 tsp red currant jelly on each noisette or chop. Place under grill, lower the heat to medium. Grill for about 5–10 minutes depending on thickness. Turn over, add more red currant jelly and grill for further 5–10 minutes.

Cut out 7.5 cm (3 in) circles of bread and fry or toast to make croûtes. Place the croûtes on a serving dish, top with a noisette or chop on each, and keep warm. Add the stock to grill pan, mix well and pour over chops.

Serve garnished with watercress and duchesse potatoes.

LAMB AND ORANGE RIBLETS

Serves 4

1 tbsp soy sauce
1 tbsp dry sherry
½ tsp ground ginger
25 g (1 oz) crystallised root ginger, finely chopped
2 oranges, rind and juice
450 g (1 lb) lean riblets or breast of lamb strips
1 onion, finely chopped
1 tbsp vegetable oil

Mix the soy sauce, sherry, gingers and the rind and juice of the oranges, and marinade meat overnight. Heat the oven to 180°C (350°F) mark 4. Fry the onion in oil until transparent. Add the onion to the meat. Turn the meat into a greased roasting tin and spread out. Bake for 1–1½ hours until meat is tender. Turn and baste meat frequently in the marinade.

Serve meat on a bed of rice or pasta.

If more sauce is required, add a little stock to meat at last basting, and this will form a gravy. Can be eaten with fingers like barbecued spare ribs in a Chinese meal and cooks well on a barbecue.

LAMB PILAU (PILAFF)

Serves 4

*450–700 g (1–1½ lb) cubed leg or
   shoulder of lamb
575 ml (1 pint) stock or water
1 cm (½ in) fresh root ginger in thin
   slices
5 cm (2 in) cinnamon stick
¼ tsp grated nutmeg
1 green chilli pepper, chopped
6 black peppercorns
150 ml (¼ pint) natural yoghurt
1 lemon, rind and juice
½ tsp cayenne pepper or tandoori
   spice mix
225 g (8 oz) long grain rice
50 g (2 oz) butter or margarine
2 tbsp oil
1 onion, finely chopped
4 cloves
4 cardamom seeds
1 onion, sliced and fried to golden
2 tbsp raisins
2 tbsp slivered almonds, toasted
2 hard-boiled eggs, quartered*

Simmer the meat in stock containing ginger, cinnamon, nutmeg, chilli, and peppercorns for 40 minutes.

Remove the meat to a bowl. Discard the cinnamon but reserve the liquor for cooking the rice. Add the yoghurt, lemon rind and juice and cayenne to the meat, stir and leave to marinade for 2 hours.

Approximately half an hour before required, fry the rice in butter and oil for 3 minutes. Remove from the fat and put in a pan with the reserved cooking liquor, the chopped onion, cloves and cardamom seeds. Cover and simmer for about 12 minutes for white and 20 minutes for brown rice. All the liquid should be absorbed, if not drain.

While the rice is cooking, fry the marinaded meat in the remains of the butter and oil until browned, and cooked through. Mix the cooked meat and rice and pile into a warmed serving bowl, top with fried onions, raisins and almonds, with the egg around the edge of the bowl.

CROWN ROAST OF LAMB

Serves 4–6

*1 crown roast of lamb (2 best ends of
   neck with 6 chops each)
stuffing of choice (1 quantity, see
   pages 87–89)*

An impressive looking dish for entertaining, which need not be very expensive. Stuffing may be in the middle, or in balls around the 'crown' in which case the centre is usually filled with vegetables.

Unless you have the correct equipment, ask the butcher to prepare the meat for a Crown Roast, by cutting through the chops at the spine end only and by chining the joint. The rib bones should be scraped clean for 2.5 cm (1 in). Bend the two joints round a jar or similar, so that cuts between chops open out. Use a trussing needle and string to tie together at the ends. Weigh the joint, place in a roasting tin, remove the jar and fill with stuffing in the centre.

Heat the oven to 180°C (350°F) mark 4. Cover the ends of the bones and stuffing with foil. When the oven is hot, put in meat and cook for 25 minutes for every ½ kg (1 lb) of meat plus an extra 25 minutes.

Remove the foil. Place on serving platter and decorate with cutlet frills, glacé cherries or stuffing balls for the ends of the rib bones. Surround with coloured vegetables (small carrots, new potatoes, courgettes etc).

Serve immediately with a thin gravy or suitable sauce (see page 12).

LAMB CHOPS WITH APRICOTS

Serves 4

400 g (14 oz) can of apricots in juice
1 tbsp red wine vinegar
2 spring onions, finely chopped
15 g (½ oz) cornflour or beurre manié (see page 90)
4 loin or chump chops, or leg or shoulder steaks of lamb
1 tbsp oil

Heat the grill. Strain the apricots and mix the juice with the vinegar, onions and cornflour. Heat and boil just before serving, for an accompanying sauce.

Brush the chops with oil and grill until tender, but still pink in the middle, about 7–10 minutes a side depending on thickness of chops. After the chops have been turned, arrange the apricots around the meat so that they heat through.

Serve the chops with apricots around, and with the sauce to hand.

BRAISED, ROLLED SHOULDER OF LAMB

Serves 6–8

1 shoulder of lamb, boned, rolled
   and tied (can be stuffed if
   preferred)
1 tbsp flour
1 tsp paprika
seasoning to taste
25 g (1 oz) butter o~ margarine
100 g (4 oz) dried ipricots, soaked
50 g (2 oz) walnı s, broken in pieces
2 onions, sliced
2 large carrots,· liced
2 stalks celery, sliced
1 stock cube
275 ml (½ pint) water
3 tbsp tomato purée

Heat the oven to 180°C (350°F) mark 4.
Dust the joint with a mixture of flour,
paprika and seasoning. Melt the butter and
fry joint to brown all round, remove and
place in a casserole dish, with apricots and
walnuts. Fry the onions, carrots and celery
to lightly brown and then stir in the
remaining flour mix. Blend the stock cube
and water, add the tomato purée and mix.
Add to the casserole dish. Cover and cook in
the oven until the meat is tender,
approximately 20 minutes per ½ kg (or
1 lb) weight of prepared joint.

Place the meat on a warmed serving
platter and keep hot. Either strain the
vegetables and use the liquor as the basis of
a sauce by adding water and thickening with
cornflour or beurre manié (see page 90), or
liquidise vegetables with liquor, and serve,
reheated, as a sauce.

LAMB AND COURGETTE SAUTE

Serves 4

450 g (1 lb) boneless neck fillet of
   lamb
1 tbsp soy sauce
2 tbsp dry sherry
½ tsp caraway seeds
25 g (1 oz) butter
2 tbsp oil
4–6 spring onions in 2.5 cm (1 in)
   pieces
50 g (2 oz) button mushrooms
225 g (8 oz) small courgettes in 2 cm
   (¾ in) pieces

Mix the lamb with the soy sauce, sherry and
caraway seeds. Heat the butter and oil and
fry the meat until browned, add the
remaining ingredients and fry, turning
periodically until meat is cooked and
courgettes browned.
   Serve immediately.

FRENCH LAMB CASSEROLE

Serves 4

700 g (1½ lb) stewing lamb, allow
  more if a lot of bone included
2 onions, quartered
1 tbsp oil
25 g (1 oz) wholemeal flour
2 cloves garlic, crushed
575 ml (1 pint) stock
1 bouquet garni
2 tbsp brandy (optional)
225 g (8 oz) pickling onions
25 g (1 oz) butter or margarine
100 g (4 oz) peas
1 tbsp chopped parsley to garnish

Heat the oven to 190°C (375°F) mark 5.
Trim as much fat off the meat as possible.
Put in large casserole. Cook the quartered
onions in oil until well browned. Stir in
flour and garlic and blend in stock, and
pour over meat. Add bouquet garni and
brandy (optional). Cover and cook in oven
for 1–2 hours, or until meat is tender.
  Fry the onions whole in the butter until
golden brown. Drain well and add to the
casserole with the peas about 15 minutes
before the end of cooking time.
  Serve with boiled potatoes and garnish
with chopped parsley.

RAGOUT OF LAMB AND BUTTER BEANS

Serves 4

2 tbsp oil
1 tbsp wholemeal flour
1 tsp herbs, chopped
seasoning to taste
½ tsp paprika
450 g (1 lb) boneless or 700 g
  (1½ lb) with bone, stewing lamb
100 g (4 oz) butter beans, soaked
225 g (8 oz) shallots or small onions
400 g (14 oz) can of tomatoes
150 ml (¼ pint) natural yoghurt

Heat the oil in a pan. Mix the flour, herbs,
seasoning and paprika together and put in
polythene bag with meat. Toss together
thoroughly.
  Fry the meat in oil until browned. Add all
the ingredients except the yoghurt to the
pan and simmer, covered, for 1–1½ hours,
or until meat and beans are tender. If very
old or tough meat is being used, cook for ½
hour before adding the beans.
  Just before serving, stir in the yoghurt,
and heat but do not boil. Serve garnished
with chopped parsley and boiled potatoes or
pasta.

If the meat is very fatty, cook the day
before, but refrigerate before adding the
yoghurt. The next day, remove the layer of
fat, reheat and finish as above.

LAMB AND BEAN HOT POT

Serves 4

450 g (1 lb) boned or 700 g (1½ lb)
  with bone, stewing lamb or
  mutton
2 onions, sliced
3 carrots, sliced
1 small turnip or swede, cubed
100 g (4 oz) haricot or any other
  beans, soaked
1 tsp mixed herbs
seasoning to taste
2 tbsp Worcester sauce
575 ml (1 pint) stock
450–700 g (1–1½ lb) potatoes,
  scrubbed and sliced
15 g (½ oz) butter, melted

Heat the oven to 150°C (300°F) mark 2.
Trim the fat from the meat where possible.
If very fatty, just cover the meat with water,
bring to the boil and simmer for 10 minutes,
then drain, discarding the water with the
melted fat.

Layer all the ingredients except the
potatoes and butter in a deep casserole. Top
with sliced potato and melted butter. Cook
uncovered for 2–2½ hours or until meat is
tender. The oven can be turned up for the
last 20 minutes, if necessary, to brown
potatoes.

This dish can be cooked in a slow cooker,
follow manufacturer's instructions for time,
and brown under a grill to colour the potato
at the end. Stewing beef, veal and poultry
can be cooked in the same way.

LAMB AND YOGHURT CASSEROLE

Serves 4

450–700 g (1–1½ lb) boneless
  lamb, cubed
1 tbsp flour
1 tsp chopped mint
ground black peppercorns
15 g (½ oz) margarine or butter
1 tbsp oil
1 onion, chopped
275 ml (½ pint) stock
1 tbsp capers
1–2 pickled dill cucumbers, sliced
1 lemon, rind and juice
1 tbsp chopped parsley or coriander
  leaves
275 ml (½ pint) natural yoghurt

Heat the oven to 170°C (325°F) mark 3.
Toss the meat in flour, seasoned with the
mint and pepper. Melt the margarine or
butter together with the oil and fry meat to
brown. Remove meat to a casserole. Fry the
onion until transparent and add to meat.
Mix in the stock, capers, cucumber, lemon
and herbs, cover and cook until meat is
tender, 1–2 hours, depending on cut used.

Remove from the oven and stir in the
yoghurt, adjust the consistency if required,
and heat through but do not boil. The dish
can be garnished with cucumber and lemon
slices.

Serve with rice, pasta or boiled potatoes
and fresh vegetables.

LAMB AND CHICK PEA CURRY

Serves 4–6

100 g (4 oz) chick peas
1 tbsp curry powder
½ tsp each of ginger, turmeric,
  paprika and cayenne pepper
1 tbsp flour
450 g (1 lb) lean lamb cubed (any
  cut is suitable)
25 g (1 oz) butter or margarine
2 tbsp oil
1 large Spanish onion, sliced
2 stalks celery
1 green pepper, cored, seeded and
  diced
25 g (1 oz) dessicated coconut
150 ml (¼ pint) milk
575 ml (1 pint) stock or water
50 g (2 oz) raisins
150 ml (¼ pint) natural yoghurt

This dish should be started the day before required for eating. Put the chick peas to soak. Mix the curry powder, spices and flour with cubed meat and leave to stand in the refrigerator, for a few hours, or overnight.

Melt the butter and oil together and fry the spiced meat until browned all over. Remove meat, and fry the onion, celery and pepper for a few minutes. Return the meat to the pan.

Boil the coconut with the milk and leave to cool, then strain and add coconut milk to the meat and chick peas along with the stock. Cover and simmer until meat is cooked, 1–2 hours depending on cut of meat, and age of animal. Stir in the raisins and yoghurt. Adjust the consistency if necessary with water or stock. Heat through, but do not boil once yoghurt has been added.

Serve with boiled rice and traditional curry accompaniments such as pappadoms, naan bread, mango and apple chutney, preserved kumquats etc. If an overnight soak and spicing is not possible, the chick peas can be brought to the boil and left to stand for an hour instead of soaking. The flavour will not have permeated the meat as well, but will still be delicious.

CITRUS LAMB CUTLETS

Serves 4

2 limes, rind and juice
1 lemon, rind and juice
2 tsp clear honey
4–8 lamb cutlets
15 g (½ oz) cornflour or beurre
manié (see page 90)
slices of lemon and lime to garnish

Mix the rind and juices with the honey and use to marinade the cutlets for a few hours or overnight if possible.

Heat the grill and then grill cutlets until cooked, but still pink in the middle, about 5–7 minutes a side. Place on serving dish and keep warm.

Make remains of marinade up to 275 ml (½ pint) with stock or water and thicken with cornflour or beurre manié. Serve the sauce over cutlets, or separately. Garnish the meat with lemon and lime slices.

Serve with chipped, jacket or duchesse potatoes.

MINTED LAMB PARCELS

Serves 4

225 g (8 oz) pastry (mixer or flaky,
see pages 92–93)
4 lamb cutlets
mint leaves
small onion, finely chopped
15 g (½ oz) butter or margarine
mint jelly
beaten egg to glaze

Make the pastry and leave in cool place to relax. Heat the oven to 220°C (425°F) mark 7. Make slits along the cutlets and lay in the mint leaves. Heat the grill and when hot, grill the cutlets for 5 minutes a side.

Fry the onion in butter until cooked and put a spoonful on each cutlet. Add a spoonful of mint jelly on top of the onion.

Roll out pastry and cut into 2.5 cm (1 in) strips. Dampen one edge with water. Wrap strips of pastry round cutlets, tucking the end underneath to seal. Decorate with pastry leaves and glaze with egg. Place on a greased baking tray and cook for 20 minutes, or until golden brown.

Serve garnished with grilled tomatoes and watercress.

SHISH KEBABS

Serves 4

Marinade
6 tbsp olive oil
4 tbsp dry sherry or vermouth
2 cloves garlic, finely chopped
¼ tsp cayenne pepper
¼ Spanish onion, finely chopped
2 tbsp fresh (1 tbsp dried) herbs
 (preferably marjoram, basil,
 oregano and parsley mixed)
ground black pepper

450–700 g (1–1½ lb) cubed lamb,
 from the leg
8 baby onions
1 green pepper, core and seeds
 removed
1 red pepper, core and seeds removed
4 medium or 8 small tomatoes
100 g (4 oz) button mushrooms

Combine the marinade ingredients and mix
with meat overnight. If marinading is done
in a water-tight, sealed polythene container,
it can be turned periodically to mix.

Parboil or fry the onions. Cut the peppers
into pieces, and tomatoes in half unless
small.

After marinading, assemble the
ingredients on skewers to give an attractive
variety, evenly divide between skewers.
Brush the skewers with marinade and grill
or barbecue until cooked, about 15 minutes.
Turn frequently and rebrush with marinade
during cooking.

Serve with boiled rice or rice salad,
chunks of granary bread, jacket potatoes or
fresh vegetables and salad.

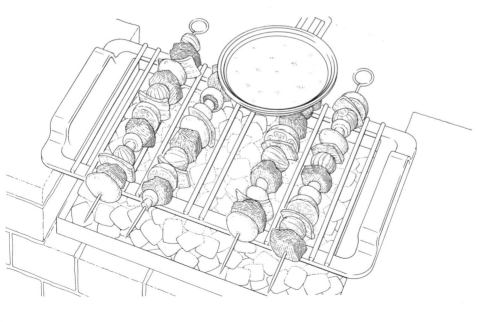

PORK

This chapter includes a wide variety of
recipes from Chinese Sweet and Sour Pork to
Mendip Oggies

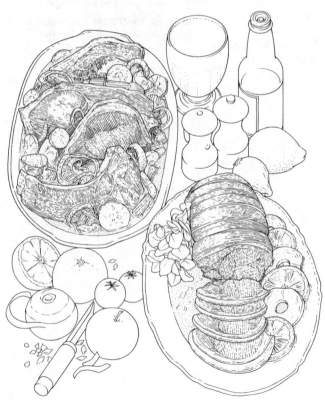

When buying, choose pork which is pale pink, firm, smooth and lean. Avoid pale watery looking meat. The fat should be firm and white. There is usually very little gristle, and increasingly the fat will have been trimmed away to give a lean product.

Although British pork is available all the year round, it becomes a particularly economical buy in the summer, when demand is traditionally at its lowest.

Cooking pork.

All joints can be roasted, grilled or fried. The forequarter cuts are reasonably priced and ideal for casseroles, stews and pies. Very little of a pig's carcase is not used for some edible item.

No attempt has been made in this book to cover the range of pork products. Recipes for pork pies can be found in *The WI Book of Pastry*.

For good crackling, ask the butcher to score the rind deeply and evenly. Brush the cut surface with oil and rub salt into the scores. Roast with the rind uppermost, in a dry roasting tin, and do not baste during cooking. The rind can be removed prior to cooking and roasted separately in a hot oven. This allows the joint to be cooked more slowly, or by a moist method, but still producing the crackling to serve with the meat.

Moist methods require the rind to be removed prior to cooking. Marinaded and frozen meat frequently do not produce crisp crackling.

Principal cuts of pork In some areas, regional names may be found

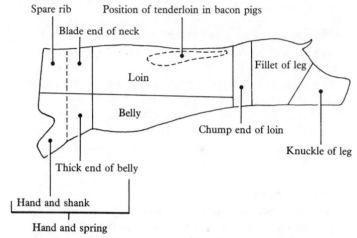

Spare rib — Position of tenderloin in bacon pigs — Blade end of neck — Loin — Fillet of leg — Belly — Chump end of loin — Knuckle of leg — Thick end of belly — Hand and shank — Hand and spring

Cuts of pork

Neck end (spare ribs and blade bone). Sometimes called shoulder of pork, this large economical joint is particularly good when boned, stuffed and rolled. Often divided into blade and spare rib (not the cut used for barbecued spare ribs which is usually rib bones with a reasonable amount of meat left on). These small cuts can be roasted, braised or stewed. Spare rib is excellent for pies and spare rib chops are suitable for braising, grilling or frying.

Hand and spring. A large joint, often divided into hand and shank and thick end of belly. Suitable for roasting, casseroles and stews.

Belly. This is a long thin cut with streaks of fat and lean. Often thickly sliced as belly strips when it is ideally grilled or barbecued to remove some of the fat. Leaner belly can be used in casseroles and minced for pâtés and sausages. The thicker end can be stuffed and rolled for a very economical roast.

Chump end of loin. Usually sold in large, meaty chops, suitable for grilling, frying or roasting. It is sometimes sold as a roasting joint.

Leg. This is usually divided into *fillet end* and *knuckle end*, both of which can be cut into smaller joints. The fillet end is the prime joint of pork and is usually roasted, on the bone, or boned and stuffed, or sliced into steaks for grilling or frying. The knuckle is usually roasted. The feet are usually removed and treated as offal.

Loin. This is a popular roast on the bone, or boned and stuffed, and it produces good crackling. It is frequently divided into chops for grilling, frying or roasting. Those from the hind quarter often contain kidney.

Tenderloin. A tender lean cut found underneath the back bone of the hind loin of bacon weight pigs, in the same position as beef fillet. In pork weight pigs the tenderloin is left in the chops, but removed in bacon pigs prior to curing. It is usually served sliced or cubed for frying, or coating with a sauce. It needs little cooking. Although quite expensive per pound it has no wastage and no fat layer.

PORK STIR FRY

Serves 4

450 g (1 lb) pork tenderloin or leg
   fillet, in thin strips
1 tbsp seasoned cornflour
1 clove garlic, finely chopped
4 tbsp oil
1 red pepper, cored and in strips
50 g (2 oz) mushrooms, sliced
100 g (4 oz) sweetcorn kernels,
   cooked
2 tbsp soy sauce

Toss the meat in the cornflour. Heat the garlic in oil in a frying pan or work, and when hot, stir fry meat until brown. Add the pepper and mushrooms, and continue stir frying until meat is cooked, approximately 10 minutes cooking altogether. Add the corn and fry to heat through.

Pour over the soy sauce and serve immediately with boiled brown rice or pasta.

SWEET AND SOUR PORK

Serves 4

450 g (1 lb) lean cubed pork
2 tbsp cornflour
4 tbsp oil
1 onion, sliced
1 tbsp tomato purée
1 clove garlic, crushed
1 tbsp soy sauce
2 tbsp wine vinegar
2 tsp clear honey
1 tbsp dry sherry
275 ml (½ pint) light stock
25 g (1 oz) crystallised ginger,
    chopped
½ tsp allspice, ground
½ star anise (optional)
50 g (2 oz) dried apricots, soaked
50 g (2 oz) mushrooms, sliced
½ red pepper, cored and sliced

Coat the meat in cornflour. Heat the oil and fry the meat until browned. Remove and fry the onion until transparent. Return the meat to the pan and add all ingredients except the apricots, mushrooms and red pepper. Cover and simmer for 40 minutes. Add the remaining ingredients and simmer for a further 10–15 minutes until meat is cooked.

Serve with rice, or as part of a Chinese meal.

PORK WITH RED CABBAGE

Serves 4

4 trimmed pork chops or shoulder
    steaks
450 g (1 lb) red cabbage, finely
    chopped
450 g (1 lb) cooking apples, peeled
    cored and sliced
225 g (8 oz) onions, sliced
2 cloves garlic, finely chopped
¼ tsp each nutmeg, allspice,
    cinnamon and thyme
black pepper
1 tsp orange rind, grated
juice of orange
2 tbsp wine vinegar
1 tbsp demerara sugar

Heat the oven to 180°C (350°F) mark 4. Grill the chops for a few minutes each side to brown. Layer the cabbage with apple, onions, garlic, spices and herbs, in a deep casserole. Add the pork chops on top.

Pour over the rind, juice and vinegar. Sprinkle sugar on top. Cover with a lid or foil and cook for 1 hour, or until meat and cabbage are cooked.

For a crisper top, remove cover for last 20 minutes cooking time.

PORK CHOPS WITH APPLE

Serves 4

4 trimmed pork chops or shoulder
steaks
small onion, chopped
1–2 tbsp oil
small red pepper, cored and sliced in
rings
200 ml (7 fl oz) apple juice
2 tbsp calvados or brandy
2 medium sized cooking apples

Heat the oven to 190°C (375°F) mark 5.
Grill or fry chops to brown the outside and
partially cook. Place in a casserole. Fry the
onion in oil until transparent, add to the
casserole, with the pepper, apple juice and
calvados.

Peel, core and slice the apples into 1 cm
(½ in) rings and place over chops. Bake
uncovered for 40 minutes, or until meat is
tender. If preferred, the cooking liquor may
be thickened with a little blended cornflour
or beurre manié (see page 90).

This dish goes well with crisply cooked
cabbage and boiled or jacket potatoes.

CASSOULET WITH PORK

Serves 4

225 g (8 oz) cubed pork
2 tbsp oil
2 cloves garlic, finely chopped
100 g (4 oz) streaky bacon, cut in
strips
175 g (6 oz) haricot beans, soaked
overnight
400 g (14 oz) can of tomatoes
275 ml (½ pint) stock
4 tbsp tomato purée
bouquet garni
1 onion, chopped
3 carrots, finely sliced
100 g (4 oz) mushrooms, sliced

Topping
4 tbsp wholemeal breadcrumbs
2 tbsp cheese, finely grated

This dish can be cooked in an oven, slow
cooker, pressure cooker, or simmered in a
pan.

If using an oven heat to 180°C (350°F)
mark 4. Fry the meat in oil to brown. Add
the garlic and bacon and fry for a few
minutes. Add all ingredients except the
topping and cook slowly until beans and
meat are tender, about 2 hours in the oven,
2–2½ hours in a pan, 30–40 minutes in a
pressure cooker, and for a slow cooker
according to manufacturer's instructions for
a similar dish.

Transfer to an oven-proof dish, add the
topping and grill or bake in a hot oven for
15–20 minutes to brown.

Serve with chunks of granary bread and a
green salad.

PIG IN THE MIDDLE

Serves 4

4 lean, rindless belly strips, chops or
  steaks
1 or 2 pigs' kidneys cored and
  quartered

Batter
1 egg
275 ml (½ pint) milk or milk/water
¼ tsp salt
½ tsp mixed herbs
100 g (4 oz) plain flour

Heat the oven to 220°C (425°F) mark 7. Lay
the meat in a roasting dish, large enough in
which to cook a Yorkshire pudding. Cook
in the oven for 10 minutes.

Beat the egg, milk, salt and herbs into
flour to make a batter.

Remove the meat from the roasting tin
and swirl fat from meat around tin. Return
the meat, add the kidneys and pour in the
batter. Return immediately to the oven, and
bake for 30–40 minutes until batter is risen
and golden brown.

Serve immediately with green vegetables
and gravy if desired.

MENDIP OGGIES (A SOMERSET PASTY)

Serves 4–6

cheese pastry made with 450 g (1 lb)
  wholemeal flour (see page 93)
450 g (1 lb) lean pork in 1 cm
  (½ in) cubes
225 g (8 oz) potato, scrubbed and
  diced
1 cooking apple, peeled, cored and
  chopped
1 tsp thyme
seasoning to taste
egg to glaze

Heat the oven to 220°C (425°F) mark 7.
Make the pastry and leave in the
refrigerator to relax.

Combine the meat, raw potato, apple,
thyme and seasoning. Divide the pastry into
4 or 6 and roll out to circles about ½ cm
(¼ in) thick. Divide the mixture between
circles.

Dampen the edges of circles and bring
the pastry up each side of the filling. Seal
and crimp across the top to give a frill
effect. Glaze with egg and bake for 30
minutes.

Lower the oven heat to 190°C (375°F)
mark 5, cover the oggies with greaseproof
paper to prevent overbrowning and cook for
30 minutes more, or until the meat feels
tender when tested with a fine skewer.

Serve hot or cold.

HONEY ROAST PORK

Serves 4–8

*joint of pork which can be on the
  bone, or boned and rolled, with or
  without stuffing*
1 tbsp oil
1 tsp salt
1 tsp ground allspice or cinnamon
4 tbsp clear honey
4 tbsp lemon juice
stuffing (see pages 87–89) to taste
*½ fresh pear per person peeled and
  cored*

Heat the oven to 180°C (350°F) mark 4. Cut the rind off the pork and rub oil and salt into the removed rind. Place in an oven-proof dish and roast at the top of the oven.

Weigh the joint and calculate the roasting time (see page 7). Sprinkle spice onto the fat of the joint, which can be criss-crossed with a sharp knife to make the fat crisp better. Mix honey and lemon and spread over joint.

Roast the meat for calculated time, basting periodically, and adding more honey if desired. Form the stuffing into balls, and bake for 40 minutes on a baking tray. For the last 30 minutes add pear halves around meat.

Serve surrounded with pears topped with stuffing balls and broken up crackling.

BARBECUED SPARE RIBS OF PORK

Serves 4–8

*450–700 g (1–1½ lb) spare ribs or
  belly strips of pork*
*2 tbsp each of soy sauce, Worcester
  sauce, tomato purée, vinegar,
  lemon juice, dry sherry and honey
  or soft brown sugar*
4 tbsp water
1 tsp garlic purée or 1 clove, crushed
1 tbsp French mustard

Heat the oven to 220°C (425°F) mark 7. Fry the meat with a minimum of fat to brown well, or roast for 20 minutes. Drain off and discard any fat.

Combine all the ingredients, pour over meat and roast (or cook in a multi-cooker/electric frypan) turning and basting frequently until the sauce is reduced and the meat is tender, about 40 minutes.

Serve as a starter, for a main meal, or as part of a Chinese meal.

PORK CHOPS OR STEAKS WITH MUSTARD

Serves 4

1 tbsp dry mustard
1 tbsp demerara sugar
4 shoulder steaks, spare rib or loin
  chops
25 g (1 oz) shredded almonds,
  toasted
seasoning to taste
tomatoes and mushrooms grilled to
  garnish

Mix the mustard and sugar together and rub into chops, or blend with a little water, and spread over both sides of chops. Grill under a preheated grill until cooked, about 8 minutes a side.

Serve with almonds scattered on top, and halved tomatoes and mushrooms around.

PORK AND PRUNE COBBLER

Serves 4–6

450 g (1 lb) lean, cubed pork
1 tbsp wholemeal flour
2 tbsp oil
1 onion, sliced
½ tsp ground allspice
½ tsp basil
275 ml (½ pint) dry cider
275 ml (½ pint) stock
225 g (8 oz) mixed root vegetables,
  diced (optional)
100 g (4 oz) prunes, soaked

Scone topping
225 g (8 oz) self-raising wholemeal
  flour (or add 1½ tsp baking
  powder to plain)
salt to taste
25 g (1 oz) margarine
bare 150 ml (¼ pint) milk or water

The stew can be made in the oven or simmered in a pan and transferred to a casserole dish to cook the 'cobbler' or scone topping. The same stew can be served with dumplings or in a pie.

Heat the oven if using to 180°C (350°F) mark 4. Toss the meat in flour and fry in oil until browned. Add the onion and fry a little longer. Stir in any remaining flour and blend in all other ingredients except the prunes. Either cover and simmer for 1½ hours or until meat is cooked, or turn into a casserole dish, cover and cook in the oven for a similar time. Add the prunes 20 minutes before the end of cooking.

Before making the topping, stir the meat well and ensure there is 5 cm (2 in) headroom in the casserole dish above the stew. Increase oven heat to 220°C (425°F) mark 7.

To make the scone mix, sieve the flour and baking powder (if used) with the salt, rub in the margarine and mix to a soft dough with the milk.

Knead lightly and using a floured board, roll out to 2 cm (¾ in) thick. Cut out 5 cm (2 in) rounds, and overlap these on top of the meat. Glaze with a little milk or beaten egg.

Bake for 30 minutes, or until scone mixture is risen and golden brown. If the meat was cold, cook for a little longer to heat the meat thoroughly. Cover scone topping with greaseproof paper to prevent overcooking.

BRAISED PORK AND ORANGE

Serves 4–6

1–1½ kg (2–3 lb) joint of pork, boned and rolled
25 g (1 oz) butter or margarine
1 onion, sliced
2 carrots, diced
2 parsnips, diced
1 chicken stock cube
275 ml (½ pint) orange juice
½ tsp mixed spice
¼ tsp Tabasco or Worcester sauce

Garnish
1 apple, cored and ringed
1 orange, peeled and sliced in rings
watercress

Heat the oven to 170°C (325°F) mark 3. Fry the joint in butter, to brown. Remove and brown the onion, carrots and parsnips. Place vegetables in a large casserole dish and place meat on top.

Dissolve the stock cube in orange juice, add the spice and sauce. Pour over meat. Cover and cook slowly for 2–2½ hours until meat is tender. Check periodically that the liquor has not boiled away, topping up with a little water if necessary.

Poach the apple and orange for a few minutes, in orange juice or water. Serve the joint with the rings of fruit around it, and with watercress to garnish.

The vegetables and stock can be liquidised and used as a basis for a sauce or gravy, diluting and thickening with cornflour as required.

PORK CHOPS IN FOIL

Serves 4

butter or oil
450 g (1 lb) potatoes, thinly sliced
1 onion, finely sliced
4 pork chops or shoulder steaks
1 apple, cored and sliced
sage leaves, chopped
seasoning to taste
4 tbsp lemon juice

Heat oven to 190°C (375°F) mark 5. Butter or grease with oil 4 pieces of foil approximately 25 cm (10 in) square. Divide the ingredients between the 4 pieces of foil, starting with a layer of potato, then onion, then the chop with apple on top. Add the sage, seasoning and lemon juice. Close up foil to form a parcel, and bake for 1 hour, or until meat is tender. For crisper, browner meat, foil can be opened up for last part of cooking.

Cooking can be speeded up by browning the meat first, parboiling potatoes and frying the onion. With this precooking, the parcels can be cooked on a barbecue in about 25–30 minutes, depending on its heat.

PORK AND LIMES

Serves 4

450 g (1 lb) cubed pork or 4 chops or
  steaks
3 limes, rind and juice
1 chicken stock cube
1 tbsp soy sauce
bunch spring onions, cleaned
100 g (4 oz) button mushrooms
50–100 g (2–4 oz) bean sprouts
25–50 g (1–2 oz) cornflour to
  thicken
1 lime, sliced to garnish

Marinade the pork in lime juice and rind for several hours. Drain and measure lime juice. Make up to 575 ml (1 pint) with boiling water. Stir a stock cube into boiling water and lime juice. Add the stock and soy sauce to the meat, and simmer slowly for 1–1½ hours until meat is tender.

Fan the spring onions by cutting down the green part. Add the mushrooms, onions and bean sprouts, and simmer for a further 10–15 minutes so that the vegetables are just cooked, but still crisp. Thicken as necessary with cornflour, blended with a little water.

Serve garnished with sliced limes and accompanied with boiled rice.

SOMERSET PORK TENDERLOINS

Serves 4

450–700 g (1–1½ lb) pork
tenderloin
1 egg
2 tbsp breadcrumbs or flour
50 g (2 oz) butter or margarine
1 large onion, finely chopped
175 g (6 oz) mushrooms, sliced
275 ml (½ pint) dry cider
seasoning to taste
4 tbsp double cream
parsley to garnish

Cut the tenderloin into 8 pieces. Place each piece between greaseproof paper and beat with a mallet or rolling pin until ½ cm (¼ in) thick.

Coat the meat with egg and breadcrumbs. Heat the butter and fry the meat for about 4 minutes a side. Remove from the pan, drain well, and arrange on a serving dish and keep warm.

Add the onion and mushrooms to the pan and fry until soft. Stir in remaining flour or breadcrumbs and cook for 1 minute. Gradually blend in the cider and bring to the boil, season and adjust consistency if necessary.

Stir in the cream, heat but do not boil. Pour over the meat and garnish with chopped parsley.

Serve with boiled or jacket potatoes.

PORK IN GINGER BEER

Serves 4

4 trimmed pork chops or steaks or
450 g (1 lb) cubed pork
2 tbsp oil
1 onion, sliced
4 sticks celery, chopped
2 carrots, thinly sliced
25 g (1 oz) wholemeal flour
1 stock cube
425 ml (¾ pint) ginger beer
1 lemon, rind and juice
225 g (8 oz) tomatoes, skinned and
quartered
seasoning to taste
2 tsp chopped crystallised ginger
(optional)

Heat the oven to 180°C (350°F) mark 4. Fry the meat in the oil, to brown. Remove and place in a casserole dish. Fry the onion until transparent, stir in the celery, carrots and flour. Mix the stock cube with 4 tbsp of water. Blend in ginger beer, stock and lemon. Pour the mixture over the meat. Add the tomatoes, seasoning and ginger (optional). Cover and cook for 45–60 minutes until meat is tender.

Serve with boiled rice or potatoes.

NORMANDY PORK

Serves 4

4 thick slices of pork (shoulder
    steaks, chops)
1 tbsp flour
½ tsp sage leaves, chopped
3 tbsp oil or 25 g (1 oz) butter
3 onions, sliced
275 ml (½ pint) dry white wine,
    cider or stock
1 tbsp calvados or brandy
3 dessert apples, peeled, cored and
    sliced
seasoning to taste

Heat the oven to 180°C (350°F) mark 4.
Coat the meat in flour mixed with sage. Fry
to brown in oil or butter and place in a
casserole dish. Fry the onions until
transparent. Add any remaining flour and
fry for a few minutes. Blend in the wine and
calvados. Pour over the meat. Add the
apples and seasoning. Cover and cook for 45
minutes or until meat is tender.

Serve with rice or boiled potatoes.

STUFFED PORK CHOPS

Serves 4

4 pork chops with bone removed
stuffing (see pages 87–89, apricot or
    apple go well)
450 g (1 lb) potatoes, scrubbed and
    sliced
1 small onion, finely chopped
¼ tsp ground mace
seasoning to taste
150 ml (¼ pint) single cream
100 g (4 oz) grated cheese (optional)
    or 15 g (½ oz) melted butter

Heat the oven to 190°C (375°F) mark 5.
With a sharp pointed knife, slit chops
almost through, making a pocket. Divide
the stuffing between the 4 pockets. Part grill
or fry to brown the chops.

Parboil the potato slices for 2–3 minutes.
Arrange the potato slices in wide oven-proof
dish, sprinkling onion and mace between
layers. Season to taste. Pour over single
cream. Lay chops on top, pushing them
down into the potatoes. Sprinkle with
cheese (if cheese is not used, brush chops
with melted butter).

Bake for 1–1½ hours until meat is cooked
and the potato soft. If the meat gets too
brown, cover with foil.

BACON AND HAM

A selection of bacon and ham recipes from
Bacon and Bean Bake to Boiled Ham and
Raisin Sauce.

Bacon is pork which has been treated with curing salts, a mixture of common salt (sodium chloride) and other permitted preservatives (saltpetre and other related substances), which give bacon its characteristic colour and flavour, and is essential for preserving the meat effectively.

Storage. Store loose bacon in the refrigerator, in 'cling-film', a polythene bag or rigid polythene container. Bacon can be kept like this for 10–14 days. Without a refrigerator, bacon will keep in a cool place for 4 days. Vacuum packs usually include a sell-by or best-before date and these should be adhered to. Once opened treat like loose bacon. Cooked ham, unless refrigerated, should be consumed within a day. With refrigeration and suitable packing, it can be kept for 2–3 days. Bacon can be frozen, although the salt in the meat accelerates the development of rancidity in the fat.

Principal cuts of bacon. In some areas regional names may be found and joints are sometimes subdivided.

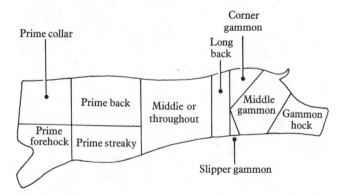

Cuts of bacon (weights where given are only approximate)

Prime back. This lean cut is normally sold as rashers, or boneless chops, which are usually grilled or fried. The chops can be baked or used in casseroles. A thick piece can be used for boiling or braising.

Middle or through cut. This is the back and streaky cut together, although in some localities it is cut into the two parts and sold separately. The through cut gives a long rasher with a mixture of lean and less lean meat and is an economical buy. It is used for grilling or a piece can be rolled and tied and used for boiling or baking, and is particularly good if stuffed before rolling.

Long back. Normally sold as fairly thin cut rashers, it is ideal for grilling or frying, but can be cubed for casseroles, pies and flans.

Corner gammon. This is a small, economical, triangular cut off the gammon, which is excellent boiled and served hot with a traditional sauce such as parsley. It is cheaper because of its rather awkward shape. It weighs about 1.8 kg (4 lb).

Middle gammon. A prime, lean and meaty cut for boiling, baking or braising whole, weighing about 2.25 kg (5 lb) but often sold as smaller joints. It can be cut into 1 cm (½ in) thick rashers for grilling or frying. *Slipper gammon* is sometimes cut from this joint and weighs about 700 g (1½ lb).

Gammon hock. Quite a high percentage of bone, especially at the lower end, but the meat is succulent and ideal for casseroles, soups and pies. Sometimes cut in half to give a reasonable boiling joint, ideal for a family meal. The hock is bought mainly for soup and stock. It weighs about 2 kg (4½ lb).

Prime streaky. These rashers combine lean with a percentage of fat in between. Look for a good proportion of lean. Excellent for grilling. Traditionally used to line pâté dishes and good for using in casseroles, pies, soups and rice dishes where carbohydrate helps to absorb the fat. A joint can be boiled and pressed. Streaky can be excellent value as it is the cheapest cut and with careful choosing can provide a filling meal, without necessarily having excess fat. Streaky usually contains little bits of cartilaginous bone, which should be cut out with scissors, along with the rind before cooking.

Prime forehock. This provides an economical meat to be cubed or minced for casseroles, meat loaves etc. It can be boiled, but is difficult to carve because of the position of the bones. Economical and weighing about 3.5 kg (8 lb) it is usually sold in smaller joints.

Prime collar. This makes an excellent joint boiled or braised as the bones are easily removed. It usually needs soaking as it can be rather salty. Collar is also sliced into rashers which are very lean. An inexpensive cut weighing about 2.5 kg (6 lb).

Cooking with bacon

Most joints are very versatile. When frying or grilling always remove the rind first. When boiling, some joints, notably the collar and hocks, may need soaking for a couple of hours to remove some of the salt. This is not always necessary with the larger, thicker joints, which today are usually less salty than was the taste a few years ago. The quick and mild cures definitely need no soaking. Where instructions are given these should be followed. Boiled joints are cooked with the rind on, this strips off easily when the meat is cooling. Baked joints usually benefit from a short period of boiling, so that the rind can be removed prior to baking. Slow baking with the meat wrapped in foil can produce a moist and succulent end result.

Cooking times
When baking, allow 20 minutes per 450 g (1 lb) and 20 minutes over for joints up to about 4.5 kg (10 lb). For larger joints only, allow 15 minutes per 450 g (1 lb).

When boiling, braising, casseroling or stewing, allow 20 minutes per 450 g (1 lb). Calculate the time from when the water comes to the boil. If using the oven, cover and cook at 180°C (350°F) mark 4.

When a combination of methods is used, the total time should be approximately 20 minutes per 450 g (1 lb). If meat has cooled down in between, allow a little for this.

BACON STUFFED COURGETTES

Serves 4

8 medium courgettes, topped and tailed
1 large onion, chopped
25 g (1 oz) margarine or butter
450 g (1 lb) collar or forehock bacon, soaked
350 g (12 oz) tomatoes, peeled and chopped (or a tin of tomatoes)
1 tsp marjoram or mixed herbs
seasoning to taste

Heat the oven to 180°C (350°F) mark 4. Cut or scoop out flesh about halfway down into each courgette and use for soup or stew.

Fry the onion in the margarine until soft. Mince or finely chop the bacon, add to the pan and stir fry for about 10 minutes. Add the remaining ingredients and mix well. Divide the mixture equally and stuff the courgettes. If there is too much filling this can be put under the courgettes while baking. Place in an oven-proof dish and cover with a lid or foil. Bake for about 45 minutes until the courgette is cooked, but still crisp.

Serve with a tomato, pepper or cheese sauce and wholemeal bread or rolls.

A marrow or squash can be used in the same way, but allow about 1 hour for cooking.

LEEK AND BACON FLAN

Serves 4–6

225 g (8 oz) quantity of mixer pastry
(see page 93)
225 g (8 oz) leeks, cleaned and sliced
100 g (4 oz) lean rindless bacon
2 eggs
150 ml (¼ pint) single cream or milk
½ tsp mustard
2 tsp chopped olives
pinch of nutmeg or mace
25 g (1 oz) grated cheese (optional)

Line a 20 cm (8 in) flan ring or dish with pastry. Prick the base and put a folded strip of foil around the edge to hold up the sides. Leave in a cool place to relax for 15 minutes. Heat the oven to 200°C (400°F) mark 6.

Simmer the leeks in a little water for 5 minutes. Cool under a cold tap and drain well. Grill the bacon and cut into pieces. Beat the eggs with the cream and mix in the mustard and olives. Place the leeks and bacon in the flan dish, pour over the egg and cream mixture. Sprinkle with the nutmeg and cheese.

Bake for 30–40 minutes until pastry is cooked and filling is set. If the filling cooks quickly, turn down the oven and cover the pie with greaseproof paper to finish cooking.

Serve hot or cold. Excellent for picnics and packed lunches.

CIDER BAKED GAMMON WITH ORANGES

Serving depends on joint size

joint of gammon
2.5 litres (4 pints) water
575 ml (1 pint) dry cider
1 onion, chopped
6 allspice berries
4 cloves
2 bay leaves

For basting
dry cider
2 tbsp demerara sugar
1 tsp dry mustard
1 tsp mixed spice or ground allspice

If the meat is a smoked or a salty joint such as collar, soak overnight. Place the joint in a large pan, sufficient to allow liquid to cover and not boil over when cooking. Cover the joint with the water and cider, add the onion, allspice, cloves and bay leaves. Bring to the boil and then simmer for 10 minutes per ½ kg (or 1 lb). Drain the joint and allow to cool a little, and cut off the rind. Score fat in a criss-cross pattern.

Heat the oven to 200°C (400°F) mark 6. Place the joint in a roasting tin and press basting ingredients into the fat. Pour over some of the cider and bake for 10 minutes

Garnish
2 oranges, sliced with rind on
glace cherries

per ½ kg (or 1 lb). Baste frequently with more mixture and more cider. When it is all used up baste from around the joint.

Remove when nearly cooked and cover with orange slices. These can be held on with cocktail sticks, but they should be removed prior to serving. Return to the oven and finish cooking. Before serving, garnish with cherries in the middle of each orange slice.

Serve hot or cold. Ideal to serve hot at one meal, and to cut cold later, which might be useful at Christmas time.

For smaller joints such as slipper and hock, reduce the ingredients to about half.

BACON AND BEAN CASSEROLE

Serves 4

225 g (8 oz) mixed beans, soaked
    overnight
3 tbsp oil
1 tsp cumin seeds
½ tsp cinnamon
bunch of spring onions, chopped
2 cloves garlic, crushed
225 g (8 oz) lean bacon, cubed
400 g (14 oz) tin tomatoes
100 g (4 oz) mushrooms, sliced
½ tsp each of ground coriander,
    turmeric and cayenne pepper
3 tbsp chopped parsley

Drain the beans and boil in plenty of water for 10 minutes and drain. Heat the oil in a large pan and fry the cumin and cinnamon for a few minutes. Add the onions and garlic and cook for 3 minutes. Add the bacon and stir fry until bacon starts to brown. Add all the remaining ingredients, reserving 1 tbsp parsley for garnish.

Return the beans to the pan and simmer gently, stirring occasionally, until beans are cooked (30–60 minutes depending on type and age of beans).

The flavour is improved if the dish stands for several hours before serving. It is excellent hot or cold. Serve with fresh vegetables, salad, pitta bread or chunks of granary bread.

BACON AND BEAN BAKE

Serves 4

225 g (8 oz) rindless bacon, chopped
1 onion, sliced
1 clove garlic, crushed
2 tbsp tomato purée
2 tbsp parsley, chopped
2 tbsp soft brown sugar
225 g (8 oz) haricot beans, soaked
black pepper
stock

Heat the oven to 150°C (300°F) mark 2. Layer all ingredients in a deep casserole and add enough stock to cover them. Bake for about 4–5 hours until the beans are soft and the liquid has been absorbed. Check periodically and add more liquid if required.

The bake can be cooked overnight in an oven at 100°C (200°F) mark ½ or in a slow cooker (read manufacturer's instructions for time).

Serve with chunks of wholemeal, or granary bread and a side salad.

HAM AND ASPARAGUS IN GRUYERE SAUCE

Serves 4

4 good slices of ham
225 g (8 oz) cooked asparagus

Sauce
25 g (1 oz) cornflour
25 g (1 oz) margarine or butter
275 ml (½ pint) milk
½ tsp powdered mustard
black pepper
¼ tsp paprika
2 tbsp cream (optional)
75 g (3 oz) gruyère cheese, grated
25 g (1 oz) wholemeal breadcrumbs
    to garnish

Heat the oven to 200°C (400°F) mark 6. Divide the asparagus between the ham slices and roll up. Place in an au gratin dish or other shallow oven-proof dish. Cover with foil. Put the rolls in the oven to heat through while the sauce is being made.

Make the sauce by heating the cornflour and margarine until the consistency is like that of a honeycomb, take off the heat then gradually add the milk. Return to the heat and boil for about 3 minutes until thick. Add all the other ingredients and stir until the cheese is melted. Do not boil once the cheese has been added or the cheese will go stringy and become indigestible.

Pour the sauce over the rolls and sprinkle with breadcrumbs. Return to the oven to brown.

The dish can be assembled and left and then heated and browned at the same time. This will take about 30–40 minutes.

This recipe can be made more economical by using cooked leeks and Edam cheese and still tastes delicious.

BAKED HAM AND STUFFED PEACHES

Serves 4–6

1.5 kg (3 lb) bacon joint
few cloves
2 tbsp clear honey
½ quantity of stuffing (see pages
  87–89 for recipes)
425 g (15 oz) can peach halves in
  juice
15 g (½ oz) cornflour

Weigh the joint and calculate cooking time (see page 67). Place the joint in a large pan, cover with water and bring to the boil. Simmer for 20 minutes. Strain, and when cool enough to handle, remove the rind from joint. Heat the oven to 200°C (400°F) mark 6.

Place the meat in an oven-proof dish. Slash the fat on the joint in a criss-cross pattern, press in the cloves, and spoon over honey. Bake for the cooking time less 20 minutes.

Meanwhile make the stuffing and shape into balls, one per peach half. Bake on a greased baking tray for 20 minutes.

Make up peach juice to 275 ml (½ pint) with water. Blend with cornflour and boil for 5 minutes until thickened. Add the peach halves and simmer to heat them through.

Serve the joint of bacon on a dish, surrounded with peach halves, topped with a stuffing ball. Serve the sauce separately. The dish should be garnished with watercress and served with fresh, coloured vegetables for best effect. It can be eaten cold and makes an excellent centre for a buffet.

BACON, APPLE AND POTATO HOT POT

Serves 4

450 g (1 lb) bacon pieces or small
  joint, cubed
1 onion
450 g (1 lb) potatoes, scrubbed and
  quartered or sliced
225 g (8 oz) mixed root vegetables
  peeled and diced
2 eating apples, cored and thickly
  sliced
1 tsp sage leaves, chopped
275 ml (½ pint) stock
275 ml (½ pint) cider or more stock
chopped parsley to garnish

Heat the oven to 180°C (350°F) mark 4. Put all ingredients in a large casserole dish with well fitting lid and cook slowly until the meat is cooked, about 1½ hours. This recipe is ideal for a slow cooker (see manufacturer's instructions for times).
Serve garnished with the parsley.

An alternative way to assemble the dish is to mix all the ingredients together except the potatoes, and arrange these in a layer on the top. Remove the lid for last 30 minutes to brown the potatoes. Soaked butter or haricot beans can be substituted for the potatoes. No thickening is required with the potatoes or beans.

BOILED HAM AND RAISIN SAUCE

Serving depends on joint size

bacon joint for boiling, soaked if
  necessary
1 onion, chopped
peppercorns and cloves

Sauce
25 g (1 oz) cornflour
425 ml (¾ pint) stock (water in
  which bacon was boiled may be
  too salty)
25 g (1 oz) seedless raisins
1 tsp Worcester sauce

Cover the joint with water and add the onion and spices. Bring to the boil and simmer for 20 minutes per ½ kg (or 1 lb) of bacon.
Just before the meat is cooked, make the sauce by blending the cornflour with the stock, adding the raisins and Worcester sauce and boiling until thickened. Remove the bacon when cooked, and remove the rind.
Serve separately as a joint with sauce, or carved in slices with the sauce poured over. One quantity of sauce serves up to 6 people. This dish is traditionally served with broad beans and carrots.

BACON AND HAM

HAM IN YOGHURT SAUCE WITH PASTA

350 g (12 oz) wholemeal pasta
25 g (1 oz) cornflour
25 g (1 oz) margarine or butter
150 ml (¼ pint) milk or light stock
150 ml (¼ pint) natural yoghurt
¼ tsp ground mace
175 g (6 oz) cooked ham, in strips
½ green pepper in thin strips
50 g (2 oz) sweetcorn kernels, cooked

Cook the pasta in slightly salted boiling water until soft, about 15 minutes. Drain well.

While the pasta is cooking, heat the cornflour and margarine together and cook for a few minutes until the mixture resembles a honeycomb. Slowly add the milk, yoghurt and mace. Add the ham, pepper and sweetcorn and heat through.

Spread the pasta around edge of a hot serving dish and heap the ham mixture in the middle. Garnish with grated cheese, breadcrumbs or a coloured salad vegetable. Serve immediately.

BACON CHOPS WITH PINEAPPLE RINGS

Serves 4

4 lean bacon chops (or gammon rashers)
1 small onion, finely chopped
15 g (½ oz) margarine or butter
1 level tbsp cornflour
1 small can pineapple rings, with juice

With scissors, cut into fat around the chop or rasher, this prevents curling up during cooking. Grill or fry the chops until cooked, about 5–7 minutes per side.

Make the sauce by frying the onion in the margarine until soft, stirring in the cornflour and cooking for a few minutes, then gradually add the juice from the pineapple.

Just before the chops are cooked, add the pineapple rings to the pan and fry or grill to heat them through.

Serve the chops on a dish, garnished with the pineapple rings, with the sauce poured over. A watercress or grilled tomato garnish goes well with this dish.

Serve with fresh vegetables and chipped or jacket potatoes.

COLD PARSLEYED HAM

Serves 4

450 g (1 lb) piece of ham, cubed
275 ml (½ pint) well flavoured stock
75 ml (3 fl oz) white wine
¼ tsp nutmeg
15 g (½ oz) 1 packet powdered
* gelatine*
2 tbsp tarragon vinegar
3–4 tbsp parsley, finely chopped
cucumber and lettuce to garnish

Simmer the ham in stock, wine and nutmeg for 5 minutes, and leave to cool. Dissolve the gelatine in a little water by heating in a pan containing 2.5 cm (1 in) of water.

Strain the ham and add the stock to gelatine, followed by the vinegar. Use some gelatine mixture to paint the sides and bottom of a 1.2 litre (2 pint) mould or straight-sided dish. Sprinkle parsley liberally around the mould and leave to set. Leave the remainder of the gelatine until on the point of setting.

Mix the ham with the remainder of the parsley and tip into mould. Pour over the gelatine. Do not stir as this will disturb the coating. Leave in a cool place to set, preferably overnight.

When required, turn out and decorate with cucumber slices and twirls, or other appropriate garnish.

PEAR, PRUNE AND HAM RISOTTO

Serves 4

225 g (8 oz) wholemeal rice
1 onion, chopped
2 tbsp oil
575 ml (1 pint) light stock
150 ml (¼ pint) white wine or more
* stock*
½ tsp basil
1 eating pear
2 tbsp lemon juice
½ red or green pepper, deseeded and
* diced*
225 g (8 oz) cooked ham, cubed
50 g (2 oz) prunes, soaked, destoned
* and halved*

Fry the rice and onion in oil, in a strong based pan, until the rice begins to brown. Allow to cool slightly and add the stock, wine and basil. Bring to the boil and then lower the heat, cover with a lid and simmer for 20 minutes, or until rice is soft, but not collapsed.

Cut up the pear and toss in the lemon juice. Mix with the pepper. When the rice is cooked, add the ham, pear and prunes and heat through stirring all the time. Pile into a serving dish and decorate with rings of red or green pepper.

Serve hot or cold. Goes well with a green or mixed salad.

MINCE

Mince is versatile and easy-to-use, make the
most of it using these recipes which include old
favourites and some that are more unusual

Always look for bright coloured, moist looking mince, avoiding that which is brown and dried with a lot of fat showing. The most usual type of mince to find is beef, but increasingly pork and, occasionally, lamb may be found. It is not necessary to buy meat ready minced. The increasing ownership of electric mixers with mincer attachments and food processors which chop the meat to mince in a few seconds, has encouraged many to buy the meat of their choice, and mince it at home. This appeals particularly to those who want very lean meat, or when less easily obtained meat such as veal or lamb are required. Purchased this way, mince is usually more expensive. The reason mince is normally so reasonably priced is that it utilises the trimmings from the carcase and the cheaper less popular cuts. This of course does not apply when you buy to mince it yourself.

Most recipes in this section can be made with any type of meat and experimentation is recommended. When a particular meat is more suitable, it is mentioned.

BURGERS (WITH TOMATO SAUCE)

Serves 4–6

Burger
450 g (1 lb) minced beef or pork
50 g (2 oz) bacon, finely chopped
2 tsp capers, chopped
2 tbsp wholemeal breadcrumbs
pinch of cayenne pepper
1 tsp marjoram
1 egg

Combine all the burger ingredients together and form into a flat, circular shape. Fry in a little oil for about 10 minutes a side, or until well browned and cooked through. Keep hot until all the burgers are cooked.

Boil all the sauce ingredients together for 10–15 minutes or until the onion is cooked and the sauce is a suitable consistency.

Serve with the burgers piled down middle

Tomato sauce
450 g (1 lb) tomatoes, skinned and
    chopped, or large tin
1 onion, finely chopped
1 tsp sugar
1 tsp basil
1 tsp Worcester sauce

of serving dish, with the sauce poured over, or in a soft burger or picnic rolls with salad, tomato and chutney inside or to taste. Garnish with watercress and serve hot with salad (mixed bean goes very well) or fresh vegetables and jacket or chopped potatoes. The sauce can be used cold for picnics and packed lunches.

LASAGNE

Serves 4

Sauce
575 ml (1 pint) milk
50 g (2 oz) cornflour
50 g (2 oz) grated cheese, preferably
    Edam or gruyère or cottage
¼ tsp nutmeg
seasoning

½ quantity bolognese sauce (see page
    81) with bacon and carrots
175 g (6 oz) lasagne or lasagne verdi
1 tbsp finely grated cheese
1 tbsp wholemeal breadcrumbs

To make the cheese sauce, heat the milk and blend the cornflour in a basin with a little water. When the milk is nearly boiling, pour onto the cornflour, stir well and return to pan and boil for about 3 minutes or until the sauce is thickened. The sauce should be a thin coating consistency. Add the cheese and nutmeg and season to taste. Heat the oven to 190°C (375°F) mark 5.

Ensure the bolognese mixture is fairly runny in consistency, adding a little water if necessary. The lasagne does not require previous cooking provided that the mixture has sufficient excess liquid for it to absorb. Arrange the meat, lasagne and sauce in layers in an oven-proof dish, starting with a layer of meat, and finishing with sauce. The dish should be fairly wide so that the mixture is not more than about 6 cm (2½ in) deep, but leave 1 cm (½ in) space at the top, or mixture will boil over.

Sprinkle on extra cheese and breadcrumbs and bake for 30 minutes or until brown and bubbling; garnish with sliced tomato. Serve with fresh vegetables or salad.

STUFFED PANCAKES WITH CHEESE SAUCE

Serves 4–6

Batter
100 g (4 oz) wholemeal flour
¼ tsp salt
1 egg
275 ml (½ pint) milk or milk and water
vegetable oil for frying

Filling
1 small onion, finely chopped
1 tbsp oil
225 g (8 oz) lean mince
3 rashers bacon, chopped
3 tomatoes, skinned and chopped
100 g (4 oz) mushrooms, chopped
1 tsp marjoram
pinch cayenne pepper
ground black pepper to taste
½ red pepper, chopped

Cheese sauce
25 g (1 oz) wholemeal flour
25 g (1 oz) butter or margarine
275 ml (½ pint) milk
¼ tsp mustard
pinch of grated nutmeg
50 g (2 oz) grated cheese, preferably Edam, gruyère or cottage
wholemeal breadcrumbs

Pancakes
Sieve the flour and salt into a bowl and break the egg into a well in the centre. Gradually add half the milk, beating it into the flour with a wooden spoon. Beat for about 3 minutes then beat in the remaining milk. Leave to stand for 1 hour if possible. Cook the pancakes in a 20 cm (8 in) frying pan. Ensure the pan is well seasoned by heating it with a little oil, then rubbing well with salt and wiping out with a damp cloth. Run a little oil around the pan, and when hot run a little batter around the pan, to cover the bottom. The pancake should be thin and lacy. The mixture may need a few tablespoons of water added to thin it down. Cook over a high heat until the pancake comes away slightly from the edge. Carefully turn over using a palette knife, or by tossing. The second side needs only about 15 seconds. Remove the pancake from the pan, and keep warm in a pile if using immediately, or spread out until cold, if using later. Pancakes freeze very well.

Filling
Fry the onion in the oil until transparent. Add the mince and bacon, and fry to brown. Add the remaining ingredients and stir fry for about 7 minutes or until all the ingredients are cooked. Divide the mixture evenly between the pancakes and roll up, placing full rolls in an oven-proof dish.

Sauce
Cook the flour and fat for a few minutes. Gradually add the milk and cook until thick. Add the mustard, nutmeg and cheese, and stir until melted. Coat the pancakes with sauce, sprinkle with a mixture of cheese and breadcrumbs and

grill until golden brown. If the pancakes and filling are cold, reheat and brown at the same time in an oven at 190°C (375°F) mark 5 for 30 minutes.

MINCE AND TOMATO PIE

Serves 4

225 g (8 oz) wholemeal mixer pastry
  (see page 93)
225 g (8 oz) mince
1 onion, chopped
25 g (1 oz) wholemeal flour
1 tsp basil
225 g (8 oz) tomatoes, skinned and
  chopped
black pepper
150 ml (¼ pint) stock
1 beaten egg

The pastry is best made well in advance and chilled. Mix the mince and chopped onion and heat gently in a pan to melt the fat in the meat. When the fat runs, turn up the heat and brown the meat. Stir in the flour and cook for a few minutes. Add the other ingredients apart from the egg and simmer for 45 minutes, taking care not to boil dry, adding more water if necessary (cooks well in a microwave oven in 10–15 minutes). Cool well. This dish can be made the day before if required.

Heat the oven to 200°C (400°F) mark 6. Divide the pastry in two and use half to line the bottom of a 20 cm (8 in) greased flan ring or foil dish. Pack in cold meat mixture. Cover with remaining pastry using water to seal. Knock up the edges by making horizontal cuts with the back of a knife, then scollop by bringing up the back of the knife every 4 cm (1½ in). Pierce the top, decorate with pastry leaves and glaze with beaten egg. Bake for 40 minutes or until pastry is golden brown and firm.

Serve hot or cold. Ideal for picnics and packed lunches.

CHILLI CON CARNE

Serves 4–6

100–175 g (4–6 oz) red kidney
beans, soaked overnight
1 onion, chopped
1 tbsp vegetable oil
350–450 g (12–16 oz) minced beef
or lamb
2 cloves garlic, crushed
1–2 tsp chilli powder (to taste)
400 g (14 oz) tin tomatoes, chopped
150 ml (¼ pint) beef stock
2 tbsp tomato purée
ground pepper to taste

Boil the soaked beans in plenty of water for 20 minutes. Discard the water. Fry the onion in oil until transparent. Add the meat and fry to brown. Add the remaining ingredients and stir well. Add the cooked beans and simmer with the lid on for 30 minutes until the meat is cooked and the beans are soft but not collapsed. Adjust seasoning and serve on or with cooked wholemeal rice and a salad.

The flavour improves if it is made the day before and kept in the refrigerator. Tinned beans can be used and stirred in 5 minutes before the end of cooking.

Red kidney beans must be boiled for at least 10 minutes before eating, to ensure any mould that *might* be present is destroyed. Once this has been done, they are perfectly safe to eat, without further cooking, in salads. Tinned beans have already been cooked during the canning process.

MINCE WITH CRANBERRIES AND ORANGES

Serves 4

1 onion, chopped
1 tbsp vegetable oil
450 g (1 lb) lean mince
25 g (1 oz) wholemeal flour
275 ml (½ pint) stock
1 tsp oregano
1 orange, grated rind and juice
75 g (3 oz) cranberries, fresh or
frozen

Fry the onion in oil over a low heat, until it is transparent. Stir in the meat, turn up the heat and brown. Stir in the flour, gradually add the stock and remaining ingredients, except the cranberries. Cover and simmer for 20 minutes.

Add the cranberries and cook for a further 15 minutes or until the meat is tender. The cranberries should remain whole, but soft.

Serve with jacket potatoes as a filling, wholemeal rice or pasta, or as a pie filling.

RISOTTO MILANESE

Serves 4–6

onion, chopped
cloves garlic, crushed
tbsp oil
25 g (8 oz) wholegrain brown rice
25 g (8 oz) beef mince
00 g (4 oz) bacon, chopped
00 g (14 oz) tin tomatoes, chopped
tbsp tomato purée
½ tsp oregano
½ tsp tarragon
00 g (4 oz) sweetcorn kernels
seasoning to taste
25 ml (¾ pint) stock or stock and
    white wine mixed
chopped parsley to garnish

Fry the onion and garlic in oil for 3–5
minutes until transparent. Add the rice and
stir fry until brown, add the beef and fry for
5 minutes. Add all the ingredients and
simmer until the rice is cooked, about 15
minutes. Alternatively the mixture can be
cooked in an oven heated to 190°C (375°F)
mark 5 for 40–50 minutes, depending on
the thickness of the dish.
    Serve hot or cold garnished with parsley.

Instead of mince any type of cooked meat
can be used. Cut it up in cubes, and stir in
just before rice is cooked, for 5 minutes
cooking.

BOLOGNESE SAUCE FOR PASTA

Serves 4

onion, chopped
tbsp vegetable oil
1–2 cloves garlic, crushed
50 g (1 lb) lean mince
tbsp tomato purée
00 g (14 oz) tin tomatoes, chopped
75 ml (½ pint) stock
tsp honey
tbsp wine vinegar
tsp basil
tsp oregano
black pepper
50–100 g (2–4 oz) streaky bacon,
    chopped (optional)
00 g (4 oz) carrots, finely diced
    (optional)
50–75 g (2–3 oz) spaghetti or pasta
    per person
Parmesan cheese, grated to garnish

Fry the onion slowly in oil to soften. Add
the garlic and meat and fry to brown. Stir in
the purée, tomatoes, stock and remaining
ingredients. Simmer in a covered pan for
about 30 minutes, adding more water if the
mixture becomes too dry.
    Meanwhile cook the spaghetti in plenty of
boiling, slightly salted water for 12–15
minutes until it is tender but still firm to
bite. Wholemeal pasta may take a few
minutes more. Fresh spaghetti is usually
cooked in about 5 minutes. The pasta may
be tossed in a little butter.
    Serve the meat piled in the centre of
spaghetti or pasta, sprinkled with cheese; it
is excellent with a side salad.

CURRIED OR INDIAN MINCE FILLING

Serves 4–8

1 tart apple
lemon juice
1 onion, chopped
1 tbsp vegetable oil
450 g (1 lb) lean minced beef or
  lamb
25 g (1 oz) wholemeal flour
275 ml (½ pint) beef stock
1 tsp each turmeric, ground
  coriander and ground cumin
3–6 whole cardomon seeds
1 tbsp mustard pickle
25 g (1 oz) seedless raisins
1 tbsp red currant jelly
1 banana, sliced

Core and chop the apple and coat in lemon juice. Fry the onion in the oil until transparent, add the meat and brown. Stir in the flour, and blend in stock. Add the spices, pickle, raisins and jelly and simmer, with lid on for 45 minutes. If mixture gets too dry, add more water.

Ten minutes before the end of cooking, add the cored and chopped apple. When cooked, stir in banana and warm through.

Serve sprinkled with coconut in hot pitta bread; pancakes, optionally with a sauce to coat them; jacket potatoes; vol-au-vents; or as a pie filling; with side dishes such as sliced tomato, grated carrot and mango chutney.

BEEF AND SPINACH MEATLOAF

Serves 4–6

225 g (8 oz) fresh spinach leaves,
  destalked
350 g (12 oz) mince (pork is
  excellent)
50 g (2 oz) mushrooms, finely
  chopped
50 g (2 oz) wholemeal breadcrumbs
1 onion, grated
1 clove garlic, crushed
1 tsp oregano
3 eggs, soft boiled (shelled) or
  poached

Heat the oven to 190°C (375°F) mark 5. Blanch the spinach in boiling water for 1 minute. Drain well. Grease a 1 kg (2 lb) loaf tin. Line the sides and base with spinach leaves, allowing them to hang over the edges, to be wrapped over when the filling is added.

Combine all ingredients except the eggs. Place half carefully in the tin, without disturbing the spinach. Make wells in the meat and place in eggs. Cover with the remaining meat, flatten the top, and fold over the spinach leaves to cover the meat.

Cover with foil or greaseproof paper. Bake for 1 hour until the meat is cooked. Turn out on to a serving dish and serve, sliced; this is delicious hot or cold and goes well with a tomato, spicy or curry sauce.

MOUSSAKA

Serves 4–6

medium aubergines, sliced
tbsp vegetable oil
15 g (½ oz) butter
large onion, sliced
clove garlic, crushed
450 g (1 lb) minced meat (usually
* lamb)*
tsp ground allspice or cinnamon
tbsp parsley, chopped
tbsp tomato purée
450 g (1 lb) potatoes, sliced and
* parboiled*
150 ml (¼ pint) water or stock

Sauce
25 g (1 oz) butter or margarine
40 g (1½ oz) cornflour
425 ml (¾ pint) milk
seasoning
* egg*

Fry the aubergine slices in oil and butter until browned on both sides. Fry in batches, if necessary using a little more fat. Remove when browned and drain on absorbent paper.

Add the onion and garlic to the pan and fry for a few minutes. Add the meat and brown, then add the spice, parsley and purée.

Make the sauce by cooking the fat and cornflour together for a few minutes, gradually adding the milk and reheating and then boiling for 3–5 minutes until the sauce has thickened. Season and when cool, beat in the egg.

Heat the oven to 190°C (375°F) mark 5. Assemble the moussaka in a deep oven-proof dish with alternating layers of aubergine, meat and potato. Add the water. Pour over the sauce, and bake for 30 minutes until golden brown.

Serve hot or cold with fresh vegetables or a salad. It is particularly good with a sliced tomato and chive salad.

MEATBALLS WITH SOURED CREAM

Serves 4–6

75 g (3 oz) wholemeal bread
150 ml (¼ pint) milk or tomato juice
350 g (12 oz) mince
2 cloves garlic, crushed
2 tbsp parsley, chopped
2 tbsp curry powder or 1 tbsp
　anchovy essence or 2 tbsp tomato
　purée
flour for shaping
oil (if fried)
150 ml (¼ pint) soured cream

Soak the bread in the milk or juice. Mash with all other ingredients except the soured cream. Form into balls approximately 2.5 cm (1 in) in diameter using flour to prevent sticking. Fry for 6–8 minutes or bake in an oven 180°C (350°F) mark 4 for ³0 minutes. Pile on to a serving dish and top ith soured cream.

Serve with chunks of wholemeal or granary bread and salad or fresh vegetables, or on a bed of buttered noodles.

BOBOTIE

Serves 4

2 onions, sliced
2 tbsp oil
450 g (1 lb) minced meat, beef or
　pork
1 tbsp curry powder
1 tsp mixed herbs
2 tsp soft brown sugar
½ tsp salt
1 tbsp vinegar
1 tbsp lemon juice
2 eggs
100 g (4 oz) wholemeal bread
275 ml (½ pint) milk
25 g (1 oz) flaked almonds, toasted

Heat the oven to 200°C (400°F) mark 6. Fry the onions in oil until soft. Stir in the meat and fry until brown. Add the curry powder herbs, sugar, salt, vinegar and lemon juice. Beat in *one* egg. Soak the bread in milk. Drain off excess milk and beat together with other egg. Beat the soaked bread with the meat mixture. Pour into a deep oven-proof dish. Pour the egg and milk mixture over the meat and sprinkle with almonds. Bake for 30 minutes, reduce oven to 180°C (350°F) mark 4 for a further 30 minutes.

Serve with fresh vegetables or a salad, with potatoes, rice or pasta.

This dish can be made with cooked meat, in which case only cook for 30 minutes.

STUFFED CABBAGE OR VINE LEAVES

Serves 4–6

225 g (8 oz) minced cooked meat
225 g (8 oz) cooked rice (75 g/3 oz)
    uncooked)
2–3 spring onions, chopped
1 level tsp caraway seeds
25 g (1 oz) cashew or pine kernel
    nuts, chopped
1 tbsp tomato purée
1 egg
20–30 small cabbage or vine leaves
575 ml (1 pint) light stock or wine
    and stock mixture
4 tbsp oil

Heat the oven to 150°C (300°F) mark 2. Combine all the ingredients, except for the leaves, stock and oil, to form the stuffing.

Blanch the leaves in boiling water until pliable, about 2 minutes. It is sometimes easier to remove cabbage leaves without them tearing if the whole cabbage is boiled for a few minutes, then a few leaves removed and the process repeated.

Divide the mixture between the leaves, ensuring there is not too much in each so that a good tight roll can be achieved. Roll up the leaves, tucking the sides in to form compact parcels. Pack closely together in an oven-proof dish, forming a second layer if necessary. Mix the stock and oil and pour over the leaves. Cover with a lid or foil and cook for 1 hour until the stock has been absorbed.

Serve hot with a sauce such as tomato, or well chilled as a starter or buffet dish.

STUFFINGS AND ACCOMPANIMENTS

This chapter shows how to make a variety of
stuffings, marinades, sauces and pastries

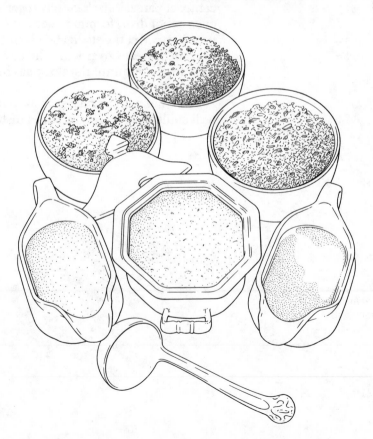

Stuffings

Stuffings, farces and forcemeats are usually based on either fresh breadcrumbs, which can be brown or white, cooked rice, oatmeal or rolled oats or starchy vegetables and nuts such as potatoes and chestnuts.

To this base can be added any ingredients to give flavour and/or succulence; these are frequently chopped onion, herbs and spices, savoury sauces and sometimes finely minced meat such as sausage meat, veal or pork, or chopped bacon rashers. Any combination can be tried. As a general rule, precook the ingredients which will not cook during the cooking time of the meat (this usually includes onion) or if by precooking, flavour or colour is added (such as bacon). The stuffing is bound together by beaten egg, milk, fruit juice, vegetable juices etc. It can be used to stuff a joint, or cooked separately.

BASIC STUFFING

00 g (4 oz) breadcrumbs, rice or
*   oatmeal*
0–100 g (2–4 oz) flavouring
*   ingredients according to type of*
*   stuffing*
–2 tbsp herbs
easoning to taste
inding ingredient

From this basic recipe most stuffings mentioned in the table on pages 12–13 can be made. Some specific recipes are given below.

BRAZIL AND DRIED PEACH STUFFING

100 g (4 oz) Brazil nuts
100 g (4 oz) dried peaches or prunes
1 onion, finely chopped
25 g (1 oz) butter or margarine
100 g (4 oz) wholemeal breadcrumbs
1 tsp allspice, ground
1 tbsp parsley, chopped
1 tsp orange rind, finely grated
2 tbsp sherry
1 egg

Finely chop or mill the Brazil nuts. Soak the peaches and then chop them.

Fry the onion in the butter until cooked. Combine all the ingredients.

This stuffing is suitable for all meats and poultry.

APRICOT AND PINE KERNEL STUFFING

100 g (4 oz) apricots, soaked and
chopped
1 onion, grated
25 g (1 oz) pine kernels or cashew
nuts
25 g (1 oz) sunflower seeds
1 tbsp fresh herbs, chopped
1 egg
seasoning to taste
25 g (1 oz) melted butter (optional)

Combine all the ingredients together.

The pine kernels and sunflower seeds can be substituted by any other chopped unsalted nuts.

VEAL FORCEMEAT (STUFFING)

100 g (4 oz) fresh breadcrumbs
25 g (1 oz) butter, melted, or suet,
shredded
1 tbsp parsley, chopped
½ tsp thyme
rind and juice of ½ lemon
¼ tsp ground nutmeg or mace
beaten egg to mix
100 g (4 oz) lean sausage meat,
minced veal or pork (optional)
1 onion, finely chopped and fried
(optional)

Combine all the ingredients and use to stuff a joint, or escalopes of meat. The stuffing can be made into forcemeat balls and baked or fried to accompany meat.

This stuffing is very suitable for lighter meats.

RICE STUFFING

100 g (4 oz) cooked rice
50 g (2 oz) sultanas
4 rashers streaky bacon, grilled and
  chopped
1 lamb's kidney, grilled and chopped
½ tsp rosemary, chopped
1 tsp lemon rind
seasoning to taste
egg or egg yolk to mix

Combine all the ingredients in a bowl with sufficient egg to bind them together.
  Use to stuff joints and escalopes, or cook in a separate dish to serve with meat.

Stuffing balls coated in egg and breadcrumbs make an unusual starter when deep fat fried and served with a tomato or piquant sauce.

WALNUT AND ORANGE STUFFING

1 onion, chopped
25 g (1 oz) butter or margarine
2 tsp ground coriander
grated rind of 1 orange
50 g (2 oz) walnuts, chopped
75 g (3 oz) raisins, chopped
75 g (3 oz) fresh breadcrumbs
1 tbsp parsley, chopped
seasoning to taste
2 tbsp orange juice
beaten egg to mix

Fry the onion in butter until soft and golden. Mix all ingredients in a bowl, with sufficient egg to bind together.
  Use to stuff pork, veal or lamb, or to make stuffing balls.

WATERCRESS OR MINT STUFFING

1 onion, chopped
25 g (1 oz) butter or margarine
50–100 g (2–4 oz) streaky bacon,
  chopped and fried (optional)
4 tbsp mint, chopped or 6 tbsp
  watercress, chopped
½ tsp ground allspice
100 g (4 oz) fresh breadcrumbs

Fry the onion in butter until soft and golden. Fry the bacon (optional). Mix all the ingredients together in a bowl, using a little milk if mixture will not bind together.
  Use to stuff joints, or escalopes of meat, especially lamb.

BEURRE MANIE (KNEADED BUTTER)

25 g (1 oz) butter or margarine
50 g (2 oz) plain flour

Knead the fat and flour together, and add small knobs to the casserole or pan, off the heat. Stir well and boil for a few minutes to cook the flour.

This is used as a liaison or thickener for soups, stews and sauces. It can be used instead of making a roux, or instead of using blended cornflour to adjust the consistency before serving.

BASIC BROWN SAUCE

1 onion, finely chopped
1 carrot, finely chopped or grated
40 g (1½ oz) cooking fat
40 g (1½ oz) flour
575 ml (1 pint) water
1 bay leaf
¼ tsp mixed herbs
seasoning to taste

Fry the onion and carrot in the fat until well browned. Stir in flour and cook for 2–3 minutes. Slowly add the water and stir well.

Add the herbs and seasoning and simmer gently for about 30 minutes. Strain and use as required, thinning if necessary for gravy, and boiling to reduce if a thicker sauce is required.

BASIC WHITE SAUCE

25 g (1 oz) butter or margarine
25 g (1 oz) flour or cornflour
275 ml (½ pint) milk for a coating
    sauce or 425 ml (¾ pint) for a
    pouring sauce

Melt the fat in a small pan. Stir in the flour and mix well. This mixture is called a roux. Cook gently for 2–3 minutes until the mixture appears to resemble a honeycomb. Remove from the heat and gradually add the milk, stirring well and heating between each addition. Boil gently for 3–4 minutes until the sauce is required consistency and smooth and glossy.

A roux can be stored in a refrigerator for a few weeks, and a little used as required to make sauces, or thicken soups and stews.

Use as a basis for such sauces as caper, mushroom, cheese, mustard, as well as sweet sauces, by the addition of the appropriate ingredients. Cream, yoghurt, sherry, brandy etc can all be beaten in just before using. Heat, but do not boil after the addition of cream or yoghurt.

STOCK

1 kg (2 lb) bones, sawn or chopped
  (do not use bacon bones)
1 onion, chopped
2 carrots, sliced
1 stick celery, chopped
small piece of turnip
1 bay leaf
bouquet garni, or bunch of herbs
4 peppercorns

Put bones in a large lidded pan, cover with water and bring to the boil. Skim off any scum if necessary.

Add all the other ingredients, and simmer very slowly for 2–3 hours, or pressure cook for 45–60 minutes. Strain, discarding bones etc and use as required.

The stock must be cooled quickly and stored in a refrigerator, and reboiled for 10 minutes before use. It can be frozen in suitably sized containers.

For gravy and some sauces a strong stock is required. For this, boil to reduce the volume and concentrate the flavour. A darker stock may be obtained by frying the bones and vegetables to brown prior to stewing.

MARINADE FOR RED MEATS

150 ml (¼ pint) red wine
2–4 tbsp vegetable oil
1 onion, finely chopped
½ tsp marjoram
½ tsp basil
1 bay leaf
dash cayenne
salt and pepper to taste
1 clove of garlic, crushed or chopped

Combine all the ingredients, and steep the meat in the marinade for at least 2 hours, turning frequently.

The remaining marinade can be used as a basis for the cooking liquor, or as an accompanying sauce. If this is to be the case, use the lesser amount of oil.

MARINADE FOR WHITE OR LIGHT MEATS

150 ml (¼ pint) white wine
2–4 tbsp vegetable oil
1 onion, finely chopped
1 carrot, in thin rings
½ tsp thyme
1 tbsp fresh, chopped parsley
1 bay leaf
½ tsp sugar
1 clove garlic, crushed or chopped

Combine all the ingredients and steep meat in the marinade for at least 2 hours, turning frequently. It can be used to baste during cooking, in which case use the greater amount of oil.

HOT LEMON AND HONEY MARINADE

150 ml (¼ pint) lemon juice
2 tbsp white wine vinegar
1 heaped tbsp clear honey
1 onion, finely chopped
1 bay leaf
1 tbsp chopped verbena, if
  available, or mint
1 tbsp fresh parsley, chopped
freshly ground black pepper
2–4 tbsp oil

Slowly heat all ingredients to boiling point. Use 4 tbsp of oil if using as a baste as well. Stir well to dissolve the honey. Pour over cubed meat and allow to cool.

This is an excellent marinade for pork or poultry which is to be barbecued. The hot marinade impregnates the meat with flavour quicker than does a cold marinade.

FLAKY PASTRY

175 g (6 oz) margarine and white
  vegetable fat mixed
225 g (8 oz) plain flour
¼ tsp salt
150 ml (¼ pint) cold water

Blend the fats together and divide in four portions. If using polyunsaturated margarine and white fat, refrigerate well before using, or use straight from the freezer, and return the pastry to the refrigerator between each rolling, for 20 minutes.

Sieve the flour and salt and rub in one portion of the fat. Mix to a soft dough with the water, knead lightly until smooth. Leave, covered with a polythene bag, in the refrigerator for 10–20 minutes. Roll out to

an oblong, about 30 cm × 10 cm
(12 in × 4 in).

Flake on a portion of fat, to cover the top
two-thirds of pastry leaving a good margin.
Fold the pastry in three, folding first the
unlarded third up, then the larded top third
down. Press edges together to seal. Cool.

Give the pastry a half turn and roll out
again, repeating the inclusion of fat and the
rolling and folding process, so that the
folded, closed edge is on your left. Continue
until all fat is used, then repeat the rolling
and folding, with no fat included.

After shaping, a better finished result will
be obtained if the assembled dish is
refrigerated for 10 minutes prior to cooking.

Cook at 220°C (425°F) mark 7 unless
recipe states otherwise. Small items take
about 15 minutes, larger ones longer,
according to fillings.

MIXER PASTRY

75 g (3 oz) polyunsaturated
    margarine
100 g (4 oz) plain wholemeal flour
100 g (4 oz) self-raising white or
    wholemeal flour
3 tbsp cold water

Using a small hand mixer, mix together the
margarine with 2 tbsp of water and half of
the flour. The mixture will resemble that of
a cake rather than a usual pastry one. Cut
and fold in the remaining flour with a little
more water only if it is necessary to make a
pliable consistency. Refrigerate well before
using.

Use and bake as shortcrust pastry at
200°C (400°F) mark 6.

For cheese pastry fold in 50–75 g (2–3 oz)
finely grated cheese, with ¼ tsp mustard
and a dash of cayenne with the flour.

WHAT IS THE WI?

If you have enjoyed this book, the chances are that you would enjoy belonging to the largest women's organisation in the country — the Women's Institute.

We are friendly, go-ahead, like-minded women, who derive enormous satisfaction from all the movement has to offer. This list is long — you can make new friends, have fun and companionship, visit new places, develop new skills, take part in community services, fight local campaigns, become a WI market producer, and play an active role in an organisation which has a national voice.

The WI is the only women's organisation in the country which owns an adult education establishment. At Denman College, you can take a course in anything from car maintenance to paper sculpture, from book-binding to yoga, or cordon bleu cookery to fly-fishing.

All you need to do to join is write to us here at the **National Federation of Women's Institutes, 39 Eccleston Street, London SW1W 9NT**, or telephone 01-730 7212, and we will put you in touch with WIs in your immediate locality. We hope to hear from you.

ABOUT THE AUTHOR

Angela Mottram, a trained Home Economics teacher, is an NFWI tutor and judge. She worked at the Meat Research Institute organising the Experimental Kitchen and Taste Panel and, while her two children were young, was a freelance Home Economist. She has now returned to teaching and lectures in Food Science and Home Economics at South Bristol Technical College.

INDEX